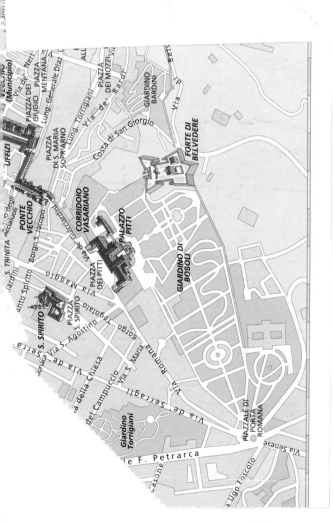

Weekend in...
Giunti Editore
Via Bolognese 165, 50139 Firenze
Tel. 0555062.1 - Fax 0555062.287
e-mail: guidgabb@giunti.it

Project Editor
Roberto De Meo

Editor
Christiane Splinter

Text
Leila Firusbakht
Loredana Melissari

Design and Layout
Media Studio, Firenze

Cover Design
Rocío Isabel González

Revision
Catherine Frost

Update
Leila Firusbakht
Loredana Melissari

Translation
Loredana Melissari

Photos
Courtesy of Apt/Firenze *(p. 7/6; p. 12/2-3: Nicola Grifoni; p. 17/4; p. 24/1: Nicola Grifoni; p. 25/4: Nicola Grifoni; p. 26/1; p. 28/1: Antonio Lelli; p. 28/3: Andrea Tradii; p. 32/2: Antonio Lelli; p. 33/4: Andrea Tradii; p. 33/5-6; p. 35/5; p. 36/2; p. 37/7: Andrea Tradii; p. 42/1: Andrea Tradii; p. 42/3; p. 43/5; p. 44/2: Nicola Grifoni; p. 45/4: Nicola Grifoni; p. 46/1; p. 49 centre)*
Courtesy of Archivio fotografico Gabinetto Vieusseux, Firenze *(p. 7/4)*
Archivio Giunti
Archivio Giunti *(Rabatti-Domingie/Firenze: p. 20/1; p. 25/3; p. 27/5; p. 44/3)*
Roberto De Meo
Loredana Melissari *(p. 49 top; p. 50 top right and centre; p. 54 centre; p. 55 top)*
Teatro del Maggio Musicale Fiorentino - Fondazione, Ufficio Stampa *(p. 73 top and bottom)*

Mapping
Stefano Benini, Firenze

www.giunti.it

© 2007 Giunti Editore S.p.A.
Via Bolognese, 165 - 50139 Florence - Italy
Via Dante, 4 - 20121 Milan - Italy
First edition: april 2007

Reprints	Year
5 4 3 2 1 0	2011 2010 2009 2008 2007

Printed at Giunti Industrie Grafiche S.p.A., Prato

Weekend in

Florence

GIUNTI

C O N T E N T S

Florence: a capital and its history

Despite having been the small capital of a very minor State (saving a brief and fairly ruinous spell as capital of Italy), Florence has a rich past, in which art and politics are closely intertwined, and has achieved moments of splendour that have spread its fame the world over.

The first settlements (4th millennium BC) are between Piazza della Signoria and Piazza della Repubblica, near a river crossing.

Florentia is born between 30 and 14 BC, a Roman colony **(1)** with the typical reticular structure: the Cardo (now Via Roma and Via Calimala) and the Decumanus (Via Strozzi, Via degli Speziali, Via del Corso) intersect near the Forum (Piazza della Repubblica). The town wall ran along the present Via Tornabuoni, Via Cerretani, Via del Proconsolo and, to the south, roughly Via Porta Rossa and Via delle Terme.

In the 2nd century AD the town expands beyond the wall. Palaces, monuments, an amphitheatre, vast Roman baths are built. During the Migration Period, however, the population declines and retreats within the wall.

In the 9th century things begin to pick up. In 1078 a new wall is built, scarcely larger than the Roman one. A third wall raised in 1173, however, includes some land south of the Arno.

In 1300 Florence has

100,000 inhabitants (Rome has fewer than 30,000, London 50,000). In 1284-1333 a new, larger wall is erected - the last. New bridges, the Bargello, a new cathedral, dazzling conventual churches are built. Local politics are stormy: now one faction prevails, now another (Guelphs and Ghibellines); more often than not, the losing party is sent into exile (among those forced to leave are Dante and Petrarca's parents). Arnolfo di Cambio is the leading architect and sculptor, Cimabue and his school prevail in painting until, towards the end of the century, Giotto appears upon the scene.

The 14th century is troubled by financial crises and plague epidemics, so that in 1427 (the year the register of real property is established) the population has decreased to 37,000. Nonetheless, great monuments are built, such as Giotto's Tower and the Loggia dei Lanzi. In 1378 social unrest leads to the Revolt of the Ciompi (wool carders) **(2)**, which is brutally put down. Oligarchic rule is established and succeeded eventually by the "signoria" (lordship) of the Medici.

In the 15th century **(3)** Filippo Brunelleschi shapes the townscape. There is a

great flowering of painters and sculptors: Donatello, Lorenzo Ghiberti, Luca Della Robbia, Masaccio, Masolino, the Beato Angelico, Filippo Lippi, Paolo Uccello, and many more. The great families leave their tower houses and build grand palaces, chief among them the Medici Palace.

Cosimo, called "il Vecchio" (the Elder) (1), is the first member of the Medici family to assume power. He is succeeded by his son Piero, and in

(3)

(1)

1469 by the latter's sons: Lorenzo (2) and Giuliano. Giuliano is murdered in 1478 during Easter Mass. Lorenzo, known as "il Magnifico", transforms Florence into a centre of

(2)

learning and of the arts. One might say that Florence still lives off that glorious age. Humanists and artists assemble at his court, among them the young Michelangelo. The century ends in an abundance of exquisite artists: Antonio del Pollaiolo, Verrocchio, Sandro Botticelli, Filippino Lippi.

Lorenzo dies in 1492. His son Piero ("the Unfortunate") manages to get himself ousted after two years. Florence again becomes a republic, under the influence of Girolamo Savonarola, prior of St Mark. His sermons against moral laxity inflame his followers, who attack women wearing finery and make bonfires of books and luxury items. Savonarola also preaches against the pope, Alexander VI Borgia, and in 1498 is burned at the stake (3). Michelangelo sculpts the David.

In 1512 the Medici are restored to power, first with Giuliano Duke of Nemours, youngest son of Lorenzo il Magnifico, then with Lorenzo Duke of Urbino. Both die young,

and Michelangelo sculpts for them two splendid tombs. This is the age of Mannerism (Pontormo).

The Medici are again ousted in 1527. Emperor Charles V lays siege to Florence for ten long months, and the republic is forced to surrender. Alessandro de' Medici becomes Duke of Florence and in 1537 is murdered by a cousin. He is succeeded by young Cosimo who will eventually (1569) be awarded the title of Grand Duke by the pope. The town is transformed by Giorgio Vasari, architect, painter, and overseer of the ducal "fabrics". Benvenuto Cellini, Giambologna and Bronzino also work for the court.

In the 17th century the house of Medici is in decline. Baroque artists such as Pietro da Cortona, Luca Giordano, Giovan Battista Foggini work in Florence, but the town is no longer the beacon of civilisation it had been.

The last Medici Grand Duke, Gian Gastone, dies childless in 1737. His sister Anna Maria Luisa, being a woman, is denied succession. She agrees to hand over Tuscany to the House of Lorraine, stipulating that her family's collections must remain in Florence for the enjoyment of the public. For this meritorious action she is remembered on 18 February, the anniversary of her death.

The first Lorraine Grand Duke is Francis Stephen, husband of Maria Theresia of Austria. He is succeeded by Peter Leopold, who pioneers reforms and opens the Uffizi Gallery to the public.

During the brief Napoleonic period (Elisa Baciocchi, one of Napoleon's sisters, is Grand Duchess), the dissolution of monasteries makes available a great number of buildings that to this day house schools and bureaucracies.

The Lorraine Grand Dukes return to power in 1814 and undertake some urban renewal, such as the enlarging of Via Calzaiuoli. Jean-Pierre Vieusseux (4), a merchant from Geneva, establishes a circulating library that becomes one of the main cultural institutions of Florence. Some young artists (Telemaco Signorini, Giovanni Fattori, Silvestro Lega) look to French painting and are disparagingly called "Macchiaioli", because they paint in "macchie" (patches) of contrasting colours.

Leopold II leaves in 1859. A year later, Tuscany votes in favour of annexation to the Kingdom of Sardinia. The 1861 census shows that at long last Florence has regained the population of 1300, and has now 114,500 inhabitants.

In 1865 Florence becomes the capital of Italy. The arrival of the royal court and of a host of civil servants unleashes the greed of speculators. Giuseppe Poggi designs an urban plan that, although only partly carried out, transforms the town: its walls are torn down, streets are widened, new quarters are built. Then the capital moves on to Rome, and Florence is left facing insolvency.

Florence's history is now part of the history of Italy. In the arts it now follows Italian trends, as in the brief Futurist season. A few artists, such as Ardengo Soffici and Ottone Rosai, are more rooted in the Tuscan past. A legacy of the 1930s are, next to some ugly Fascist buildings, the stadium by Pier Luigi Nervi (1932), and the "S. Maria Novella" Station by Giovanni Michelucci (1933-35).

Florence is liberated on 11 August 1944. The retreating Germans blow up all the bridges (5), except Ponte Vecchio, razing instead the adjoining streets, with all their ancient towers and palaces. The postwar reconstruction is less than satisfactory.

Florence is dealt another hard blow by the flood of 4 November 1966 (6). Many works of art still await restoration; many more, together with an untold number of books, are lost forever.

(5)

(6)

Useful Information

Tourist Information Centres

Via Cavour 1/r,
tel 055.290832-3,
infoturismo@provincia.fi.it
8.30am-6.30pm,
Sun 8.30am-1.30pm
Via Manzoni 16,
tel 055.23320,
info@firenzeturismo.it
Mon-Fri 9am-13pm
Borgo Santa Croce 29/r,
tel 055.2340444,
turismo2@comune.fi.it
9am-7pm (winter 9am-6pm),
Sun 9am-2pm
Aeroporto "A. Vespucci",
tel 055.315874, infoaeroporto
@aeroporto.firenze.it
8.30am-8.30pm
Piazza Stazione 4/a,
tel 055.212245,
turismo3@comune.fi.it
8.30am-7pm, Sun 8.30am-2pm

Airport

"Amerigo Vespucci",
tel 055.30615 (switchboard),
055.3061700-702 (flight
info, 6am-midnight)
www.aeroporto.firenze.it
Ticket Office: 5.10am-7am
5 km (3.1 miles) from the
town centre, the airport can
be reached by taxi (approx.
15/20 €) or by shuttle bus
"Vola in bus" from SITA
Coach Station (Via S. Cateri-
na da Siena, adjoining S. M.
Novella Railway Station): dep.
every 30 min (6am-11.30pm
from the airport; 5.30am-
11pm from the coach sta-
tion); journey time approx. 25
min; tickets (4 €) on the bus.

Railway Stations

Santa Maria Novella,
Piazza Stazione 1
Ticket Office: 5.45am-10pm

Telephone bookings:
tel 199.166177 (8.30am-
8pm) (tickets at the station)
Left Luggage: 6am-12 midnight
(up to 5 hours: 3.80 €; 6th to
12th hour: 0.60 € per hour;
from the 13th hour on:
0.20 € per hour)
Campo di Marte,
Via Mannelli 12
Ticket Office: 6.20am-9pm
Rifredi, *Via dello Steccuto 1*
Ticket Office: 6.30am-8pm

Bus

There is an extensive network
of public buses. Tickets –
varying in validity and price –
can be purchased from tobac-
conists, licensed retailers displaying a special sticker, and
some parking meters; they
can also be bought on board
for 2 € (no change is given by
the driver). All tickets must be
validated on the bus.
Info **Box ATAF**, Piazza
Stazione (7.15am-7.45pm);
freephone 800 424500
(6am-9pm), *www.ataf.net.*
The "Iris Ticket" gives unlim-
ited travel on trains and
buses in the provinces of
Florence and Prato and also

offers discounts for mu-
seums and other services. It
can be purchased from railway ticket offices (at stations
or licensed retailers) and
from tourist offices: 1 day
8 € (children 4-12: 5 €) or
3 days 23 € (12 €).
City Sightseeing Firenze pro-
vides live guided tours of the
city on red double-decker
buses, as in London. Info at
some hotels and at the starting point next to S.M. Novella
Station. Runs every 30 min,
from 9am to 7pm (Jun-Aug
9am-11pm); Journey time:
60 min. The new **Firenze
PassePartour** card is valid 24
hours for travelling on all ATAF
(public transport) and City
Sighseeing buses (22 €;
under 15s: 11 €).

Taxi

Cabs can be boarded at taxi
stands (S.M.N. Station, behind the apse in Piazza Duomo, Piazza della Repubblica,
Piazza S. Marco, among
others), or by ringing Radio-
taxi: *tel 055.4390-055.4499,*
or *055.4798-055.4242.*

Getting around by car

The best advice is: do not at-
tempt to drive in Florence.
Non-residents may enter the
Limited Traffic Zones (ZTL)
only in order to reach their

Red Numbers

Florence has a unique numbering system, with red numbers for businesses and black (or blue) numbers for houses. The two series proceed independently. One more tip to help you find your way: in streets perpendicular to the Arno, numbers start at the end of the street closest to the river, whereas in streets parallel to the river they start upstream.

hotel or a garage (waiting inside the zones is not allowed in any case). The car parks in Piazza della Libertà (Parterre) and Piazza della Calza (Porta Romana) offer tourist discount rates: approx. 15 € for 24 hours, and lower rates for overnight parking.

Other car parks (open 24 hours): S.M.N. Station, S. Ambrogio (Piazza Ghiberti), Piazza Beccaria, Fortezza. Info: *www.firenzeparcheggi.it* Towed away vehicles: *Viadotto all'Indiano, loc. Ponte a Greve, tel 055.783882 (open 24 hours).*

Bicycles and electric vehicles for hire

Along the narrow streets of the city centre, many of which have been pedestrianised, the best vehicle, and often the only one allowed, is a bicycle. To hire one:
Alinari *Via Guelfa 85r, tel 055.280500*
Florence by Bike *Via S. Zanobi 120-122/r, tel 055.488992*
"Mille e una bici" is a municipal service that enables people to rent a bike at bargain rates. Bike stands: S.M. Novella Station, Parterre, Campo di Marte Station, Piazza Ghiberti, Piazza Cestello, Piazza Vittorio Vene-

to. Opening times: 7.30am-7pm (may vary). An identity document is required and bikes must be returned on the same day at any bike stand, or a fine will be charged.
Rate: 1.50 € (1 hour), 4 € (5 hours) or 8 € (all day).
To rent two or four-wheeled electric vehicles that can enter ZTLs and car-free zones:
Sologiallo *Via del Ponte Sospeso 8a, tel 055.714854* (electric bikes and two or four-seat cars that may or may not require a driving licence).
At the Parterre Car Park there are 20 two-seat electric vehicles available to people who park their car (3 € per hour, 6 hours: 15 €).

Medical Help

Guardia Medica Turistica - Misericordia *Piazza Duomo (at the corner of Via Calzaiuoli), tel 055.212221 (Mon-Fri 2-6pm; surgery fee: 25 €)*
Accident and Emergency (open 24 hours):
Ospedale S.M. Nuova *Piazza S.M. Nuova 1, tel 055.27581*
Ospedale Careggi *Viale Pieraccini 17, tel 055.7949644* (also has an emergency service for eye problems)
24 hour Paediatric First Aid and Emergency: **Ospedale Meyer,** *Via Giordano 13 (about to be relocated), tel 055.56621*

24 Hour Pharmacies

Molteni *Via Calzaiuoli 7r*
All'insegna del moro *Piazza San Giovanni 20r*
Comunale 13 *S.M. Novella Station*
Info on open pharmacies: tel 800.420707

Timed museum tickets

Firenze Musei has two book-

ing offices (at the Uffizi Gallery and at Pitti Palace, Tue-Sun 8.30am-7pm) and a telephone booking service (tel 055.294883, Mon-Fri 8.30am-6.30pm, Sat 8.30am-12.30pm) that allows visitors to jump the long queues at state museums (Uffizi Gallery, Galleria dell'Accademia, Galleria Palatina, Boboli Gardens and Museo degli Argenti, Galleria d'Arte Moderna and Galleria del Costume, Medici Chapels, Museo di San Marco, Bargello, Archaeological Museum, Opificio delle Pietre Dure, booking fee 3 €). For temporary exhibitions, tickets can be booked also by ringing 055.2654321.

Florence on the Internet

Tourist Board: *www.firenzeturismo.it*
Municipality of Florence: *www.comune.fi.it* (has info also on municipal museums)
State museums: *www.polomuseale.firenze.it www.firenzemusei.it*
History of Florence: *www.storiadifirenze.org*

THE HEART

ur visit starts from the very heart of Florence, from its civic and religious centre, its cathedral and its municipal palace, connected by one of its most elegant – and busy – streets. Crowded within a small area are most of the monuments that have made Florence famous the world over and that appear in

KEY

1. Basilica di Santa Maria del Fiore (Duomo)
2. Campanile di Giotto
3. Museo dell'Opera del Duomo
4. Battistero
5. Chiesa di Orsanmichele
6. Piazza della Repubblica
7. Palazzo Strozzi
8. Basilica di Santa Trinita
9. Piazza della Signoria
10. Palazzo Vecchio (or della Signoria)
11. Galleria degli Uffizi
12. Ponte Vecchio

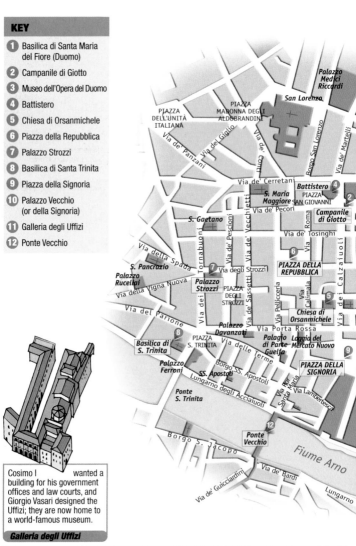

Cosimo I wanted a building for his government offices and law courts, and Giorgio Vasari designed the Uffizi; they are now home to a world-famous museum.

Galleria degli Uffizi

OF FLORENCE

all ancient views of the town: the Duomo, with its towering dome, the Baptistery, called by Dante "my beautiful San Giovanni", Giotto's Bell Tower, slender and colourful, and the Old Bridge, always a favourite with photographers.

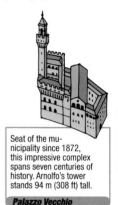

Seat of the municipality since 1872, this impressive complex spans seven centuries of history. Arnolfo's tower stands 94 m (308 ft) tall.

Palazzo Vecchio

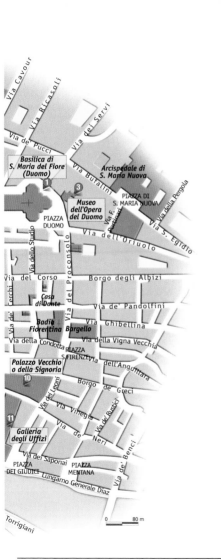

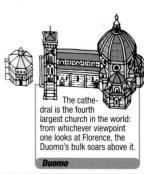

The cathedral is the fourth largest church in the world: from whichever viewpoint one looks at Florence, the Duomo's bulk soars above it.

Duomo

(1)

1. Basilica di Santa Maria del Fiore (Duomo)

Piazza Duomo
Tel 055.2302885
Mon-Fri 10am-5pm (Thu 10am-3.30pm); Sat 10am-4.45pm (1st Sat of month 10am-3.30pm); Sun and holidays 1.30-4.45pm; entrance free
Cupola *Mon-Fri 8.30am-7.00pm; Sat 8.30am-5.40pm (1st Sat of each month 8.30am-4.00pm); closed Sun and holidays; last ticket sold 40 min before closing; ticket 6 €*
Crypt *10am-5pm, Sat. 10am-4.45pm (1st Sat of month 10am-4pm) Closed Sun and holidays; ticket 3 €*

From whichever viewpoint one looks at Florence, the huge bulk of the cathedral soars above the town **(1)**. It is of a truly majestic size (the fourth largest church in the world), the confident undertaking of a town at the height of its expansion. Building was begun in 1296 by Arnolfo di Cambio and went on for one and a half centuries.

In 1368, while it was still in progress, the church was redesigned on a larger scale by Francesco Talenti (1368): from the outside one sees clearly that the bays closer to the façade are smaller. The dome, designed by Filippo Brunelleschi, was an unprecedented architectural feat, its double-walled structure self-supporting during construction. The marble gallery (1502-1515) at the base of the dome was never completed, after Michelangelo sneeringly called it a "cricket cage". The unfinished 14th-century façade was dismantled in 1587; the present, less than memorable façade by Emilio de Fabris was built in 1871-87. The vast interior **(2)**, in typically restrained Florentine Gothic style, looks bare. Several of the original stained-glass windows survive, many are

by Lorenzo Ghiberti. On the left wall are the portraits of two *condottieri*: *Niccolò da Tolentino* by Andrea del Castagno (1456) and *Giovanni Acuto* (the English mercenary John Hawkwood) by Paolo Uccello (1436), also the well-known painting by Domenico di Michelino, *Dante and the Three Realms of the Comedy* **(3)** (1465). The dome frescoes, representing the *Last Judgement*, are by Giorgio Vasari and Fede-

(2)

rico Zuccari (1572-79): recently restored, they are impressive, but not exactly a pinnacle of art. The panorama from the dome's summit (after 463 challenging steps) is breath-taking. From the right aisle a few steps lead to the crypt with the remains of the ancient

(3)

cathedral of Santa Reparata and of Roman buildings, Medieval tombstones, and most importantly the tomb of Filippo Brunelleschi (1446).

2. Campanile di Giotto

Piazza Duomo
Tel 055.2302885
8.30am-7.30pm, ticket 6 €

The building of the bell tower **(4)** was begun in 1334 by Giotto, carried on by Andrea Pisano (1337-1348), and ended in 1359 by Francesco Talenti. Its lowest level is decorated with bas-reliefs in hexagonal panels by Andrea Pisano (*Stories from the Bible* and *Human Works by Man*) and Luca della Robbia; the next level with lozenge-shaped panels depicting the *Planets*, *Virtues*, *Liberal Arts* and *Sacraments*, by Andrea Pisano and his school; the upper level has statues of *Patriarchs*, *Kings*, *Sibyls* and *Prophets*, by Andrea Pisano, Nanni di Bartolo and Donatello (originals in the Museo dell'Opera del Duomo).

Lo Scoppio del Carro

The ceremony of the "exploding wagon" is probably a pagan ritual that at some time became associated with the story of Pazzino de' Pazzi who went to the first crusade and brought back some stone fragments from the Holy Sepulchre. These are used each year on Easter Day to light a fire, which is then carried in a brazier from the church of SS. Apostoli to the cathedral. Meanwhile, a huge wagon called Brindellone (the Slob) is pulled through the streets by two oxen, attended by a colourful pageant, and is placed in front of the Duomo. During High Mass the archbishop lights with the "sacred fire" a rocket hidden inside a figurine representing a white dove, the Colombina **(5)**. Sliding on a wire, the dove reaches the wagon and lights the fireworks that cover it.

(5)

The tower is 84 m (277 ft) high; 414 steps lead to the terrace and to a stunning view.

3. Museo dell'Opera del Duomo

Piazza Duomo 9
Tel 055.2302885
Mon-Sat 9am-7.30pm; Sun and holidays 9am-1.40pm (last ticket sold 40 min before closing) ticket 6 € (under 7s free)

The museum, behind the Duomo, is home to works of art from the cathedral, Giotto's Tower and the Baptistery, displayed to great effect and with excellent explanatory panels. On display from the Duomo are the sculptures from the original Gothic façade, the two cantorial pulpits by Donatello (1433-39) and Luca della Robbia (1431-38), as well as Michelangelo's unfinished *Pietà* (1550-53).

The Misericordia

A row of ambulances parked close to Giotto's tower marks the seat of the Venerabile Arciconfraternita della Misericordia (the Venerable Confraternity of Mercy) **(6)**, a highly regarded Florentine volunteer organisation founded in 1244 to assist the sick and bury the dead. Nowadays the confraternity is engaged in a great many activities. In the Oratory (left door) are a ceramic glaze by Andrea della Robbia and a St Sebastian by Benedetto da Maiano (1485-97). On the upper floor a small museum displays works of art from bequests and donations.

(6)

(4)

(1)

24), with *Stories from the New Testament, Church Fathers* and *Evangelists*, are equally beautiful. The interior is clad in marble with inlaid geometrical patterns. Some of the columns were taken from Roman buildings. The 13th-century mosaic ceil-

Among the statues removed from the bell tower is Donatello's amazing *Habacuc*, known as "lo Zuccone" (the Bonehead); also by Donatello is the wooden sculpture of Mary Magdalene, formerly in the Baptistery. In the courtyard are the original panels from the Gates of Paradise and the group of statues *The Baptism of Christ* **(1)** by Andrea Sansovino (1502), also from the Baptistery. The wooden models of the cathedral and the various drawings for the new façade, dating from the 16th century onward, are fascinating.

Door (Porta del Paradiso, i.e. Gates of Paradise) **(3)**, Ghiberti's masterpiece (1425-52), whose panels depicting *Stories from the Old Testament* display a marvellous sense of perspective. The South Door (1330) by Andrea Pisano, with *Stories from the Life of the Baptist* and allegories of *Virtues*, and the North Door, also by Lorenzo Ghiberti (1403-

(3)

4. Battistero

Piazza S. Giovanni
Tel 055.2302885
Mon-Sat 12-6.30pm; Sun and
holidays 8.30am-1.30pm;
Closed 1 Jan, Easter, 8 Dec
and Christmas. Ticket 3 €

The Baptistery is one of the oldest monuments of Florence, so ancient that in the Middle Ages it was believed to be a Roman temple. First recorded in 897 AD, it goes back in its present form **(2)** to the 11th century. It owes its world fame to the East

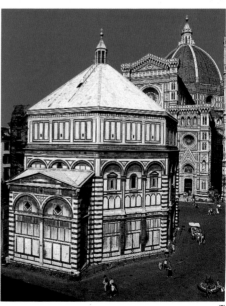

(2)

ing, depicting stories from Genesis, of Mary and Jesus, of the Baptist, and the stunning Last Judgement with the enthroned Christ, are the work of Venetian and Florentine artists, Cimabue and Coppo di Marcovaldo among them. At the corner of Via Calzaiuoli, the charming **Loggia del Bigallo** (1352-58) houses a tiny museum of sacred art (*tel 055.215440, open 10am-6pm, closed Tue, ticket 2 €*).

5. Chiesa di Orsanmichele

Via Arte della Lana
Tel 055.23885
Tue-Sun 10am-5pm, entrance free. 1st floor museum temporarily closed

The peculiar, rectangular ground plan is a reminder that this was originally a market, with a loggia at ground level and grain store-

The "Porcellino"

The so-called Mercato del Porcellino (Piglet Market) under the Loggia del Mercato Nuovo (1547-51) has long been a favourite with tourists. The "piglet" is in fact a wild boar **(5)**, a bronze copy by Pietro Tacca (1612) of the Hellenistic marble statue in the Uffizi: the small fountain on the south side of the market has been elected the Trevi Fountain of Florence by tourist who trustfully throw their coins into it. What most of them don't know is that in order to bring them luck the coin has to drop through the grating from the boar's nose (that's why it is so shiny!).

(5)

houses above. The loggia was bricked up in 1367-1380, and Orsanmichele (S. Michele in Orto, i.e. St Michael in the Kitchen Garden) **(4)** became the church of the crafts and trade guilds, which embellished the outer walls with statues of their patron saints. Most noteworthy are: on the side facing Via de' Calzaiuoli

Verrocchio's *The Disbelief of St Thomas* (1483); towards Via dell'Arte della Lana Ghiberti's *St Stephen* (1426); towards Via Brunelleschi the *Four Crowned Martyrs* (1403), by Nanni di Banco, and Donatello's *St George* (all copies). Inside there is a dazzling tabernacle (1355-59) by Andrea dell'Orcagna, encasing Bernardo Daddi's panel painting of the *Madonna delle Grazie*.

6. Piazza della Repubblica

The square, ringed by open-air cafés, was built on the site of the medieval Mercato Vecchio, that rose on the site of the Roman Forum, and of an earlier prehistoric settle-

The "Fuochi di S. Giovanni"

St John is the patron saint of Florence. His day (24 June) is a local holiday, and ends at night with the "fuochi" (fires), i.e. a fireworks display on Piazzale Michelangelo: the throng on the banks of the Arno surpasses belief.

(4)

(1)

"A vita nuova restituito"

On the arch between Piazza della Repubblica and Via Strozzi an inscription triumphantly proclaims that the town centre has been "to new life restored": some have called the "regeneration" of the Mercato Vecchio area in accordance with 19th-century ideas of decorum "the greatest crime in urban planning" of the age. Dozens of medieval towers, several ancient churches, and the entire Old Ghetto with its synagogues (3) were demolished. Traces of the historic and prehistoric past, which abounded below ground, were irretrievably lost. So the town acquired its fine "parlour", today "embellished" by souvenir stalls with the obligatory footballers' shirts. To get an idea of what Medieval Florence was like, walk around the 'chiassi' (alleys) between Via delle Terme and Borgo SS. Apostoli.

(3)

ment. An 8th-century BC necropolis was discovered during excavations for the building of the Gambrinus Theatre in the Via Brunelleschi, adjoining the square. The Colon-na dell'Abbondanza (Column of Bounty) (1) is topped by an 18th-century copy of a statue by Donatello.

7. Palazzo Strozzi
Via Strozzi

A statement of power by one of the great noble families of Florence, this awe-inspiring *palazzo* (2) was begun in 1489 by Benedetto da Maiano and completed by Cronaca (1502-3), who designed the courtyard and the massive cornice (left unfinished). On the outer walls are some remarkable wrought-iron lanterns and rings; the palace is home to several cultural institutions and is used for major temporary exhibitions.

8. Basilica di Santa Trinita
Piazza S. Trinita
Tel 055.216912 - 9am-noon 3.30-6pm; closed Sun and holidays, entrance free

Built in the late 11th century, enlarged in the 14th, and much altered in the 17th, the Basilica of the Holy Trinity retains

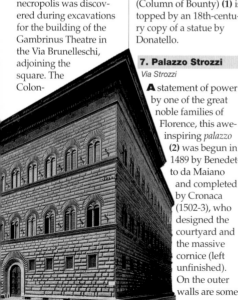

(2)

Palazzo Davanzati
Museo della casa fiorentina antica

*Via Porta Rossa 13
Tel 055.2388610
(8.15am-1.50pm;
closed 1st, 3rd and
5th Mon, 2nd and 4th
Sun of the month;
entrance free)*
The museum in this
14th-century palace
(rather fancifully refurbished in the early 20th
century) re-creates a
wealthy Florentine mansion of the 14th-15th century **(4)**. Only the ground floor and a few upper rooms are open to visitors. **(4)**

traces of 14th-century decoration and some great works of art, such as the chapel painted by Lorenzo Monaco with *Stories of the Virgin* (1420-25), and most importantly the Sassetti Chapel, with frescoes by Domenico Ghirlandaio (1483-86) showing views of Florence and portraits of contemporary personages. The 16th-century façade is by Bernardo Buontalenti, but the counter-façade is still in part the original 11th-century one.

Chiesa dei SS. Apostoli

Piazzetta del Limbo
A plaque on the façade of the Church of the Holy Apostles claims that it was founded by Charlemagne in 807: that's a legend, albeit a fascinating one. The present church goes back to the 12th century, and in the course of time has suffered many floods and subsequent repairs. It still has the ancient "cocciopesto" (crushed terracotta) floor and a fine 14th-century tie-beam roof; the glazed terracotta tabernacle is by Giovanni della Robbia. In the first chapel on the left is the 14th-century brazier used for carrying the fire for the "Scoppio del Carro" on Easter morning.

Ponte S. Trinita

The Holy Trinity Bridge was the last of the Medieval bridges. Twice swept away by a flood, it was rebuilt with higher arches by Bartolomeo Ammannati in 1567-69, and embellished with statues of the four seasons in 1608. The Germans destroyed it in 1944, but it was rebuilt in 1952 according to the original drawings. The statues were retrieved from the river.

9. Piazza della Signoria

The massive bulk of the Palazzo della Signoria, also called Palazzo Vecchio, towers over the square. The statues on the palace steps all have symbolic significance, recalling the freedom and power of Florence. The Marzocco (Donatello's original is in the Bargello), i.e. the lion holding the heraldic shield of Florence, is the city's emblem. Also on the steps are Donatello's *Judith and Holofernes* (c 1460, the original is inside, in the *Sala dei Gigli*), Michelangelo's *David* (the original is in the Galleria dell'Accademia), and Baccio Bandinelli's *Hercules and Cacus* (1534). In front of the steps a plaque in the paving marks the spot where Girolamo Savonarola and two of his associates were burnt at the stake: on the anniversary of their death, 23 May, the plaque is covered with flowers in a touching ceremony called "la Fiorita".
The **Loggia della Signoria** (also called "dell'Orcagna", because wrongly attributed to that artist, or more commonly "dei Lanzi", having been used in the 16th century as guardroom by the Landsknechts) was built in 1376-1382 as a venue for civic ceremonies. In time it has become a veritable open-air

museum, displaying statues such as Benvenuto Cellini's celebrated *Perseus* **(5)** (1554), Giambologna's *Rape of the Sabine Women* (1583) and

(5)

Hercules Beating the Centaur Nessus, Menelaus Supporting the Body of Patroclus (ancient copy of a Greek original) and Pio Fedi's *Rape of Polyxena* (1866). The Piazzale degli Uffizi opens on the right, between the palace and the Loggia dei Lanzi **(1)**. On the left is Bartolomeo Ammannati's Fountain of Neptune (1563-75). Florentines have always been critical of this marble giant, sneeringly calling it "Biancone" (Big White One). The equestrian statue of Cosimo I **(2)** (1594) is by Giambologna; the ancient building behind it is the Tribunale della Mercatanzia (1359), the

(1)

10. Palazzo Vecchio (or della Signoria)

Piazza della Signoria
Tel 055.2768465
9am-7pm; Thu and midweek holidays 9am-2pm, closed 1 and 6 Jan, Easter, 1 May, 15 Aug, 25 Dec
Tickets 6 €, concessions 4.50 €, children 2 €, family tickets available
Joint ticket with Chiesa del Carmine and Cappella Brancacci 8 €, concessions 6 €, children 3 €

Seven centuries of history are encompassed by this massive complex **(3)**, topped by the 94 m (308 ft) Torre di Arnolfo. Its core, built in the late 13th and early 14th century, and most likely designed by

Arnolfo di Cambio, was the seat of the Priori delle Arti. Enlarged in the 15th and 16th century, it became the seat of the Signoria and, in 1540, ducal residence. Cosimo I directed Vasari to transform the interiors, to make them worthy of a princely mansion. In 1565 the ducal family moved to Palazzo Pitti, and from then on the Palazzo della Signoria was called Palazzo Vecchio (Old Palace). While

(2)

guilds' law court; no. 7 is the 16th-century Uguccioni Palace; opposite Palazzo Vecchio, where once an ancient church and medieval houses used to be, stands now a mock-Renaissance palace (1871).

(3)

(4)

Florence was the capital of Italy (1865-71), it housed the Lower House. Since 1872 it has been the seat of the municipality.

The first courtyard was

A palace reveals its secrets

For those who wish to learn more about Palazzo Vecchio and its history, there is a wide range of "activities". Take a guided tour with a costumed guide and discover places that are not usually accessible: doors hidden behind paintings, secret chambers and stairways, small windows from which one can spy on others and not be seen... Even small children (3 years +) can explore the palace's secrets and experience marvellous adventures especially devised for them. Older children can attend workshops on fresco painting, learn the secrets of perspective, or experience "live" the **Renaissance in Florence**.

(Booking required. Info on tours and "activities" in English: Mon-Sun 9am-6pm next to the ticket office or by ringing 055.2768224/2768558. Each "activity" costs 6 €; ticket holders to Palazzo Vecchio only: 2 €).

redone by Michelozzo in 1439-54 and decorated with stuccowork by Vasari in 1565. The fountain is topped by Andrea del Verrocchio's *Winged Boy with a Dolphin*, (1476, the original is inside, on the *Terrazza di Giunone*). After buying tickets at the counter in the second courtyard, called "della Dogana", one can ascend the staircase to the *Quartieri Monumentali*. The visits starts with the Salone dei Cinquecento **(4)**, built in 1495, at the time of the Republic. In 1563-65 Vasari raised the ceiling, decorating it with 42 celebratory panels, with the apotheosis of Cosimo I at the centre. To the right of the entrance one can peek into Francesco I's *Studiolo*, whose walls are covered with painted panels. Opposite is Michelangelo's unfinished *Genius of Victory*. Adjoining the Salone are the *Quartieri Nuovi*, decorated by Vasari and his helpers. Only the Sala Leone X is open to the public. On the second floor are

the *Quartiere degli Elementi* and the apartments of Eleanor of Toledo, decorated with stories of famous women. The chapel of the latter is generally considered Bronzino's masterpiece. Through the ancient *Cappella dei Priori*, redone in 1511-1514, one enters the *Sala delle Udienze* and the *Sala dei Gigli*, both with exquisitely decorated ceilings. Another of the palace's treasures is the *Sala delle Carte Geografiche*, with the largest world globe of the times (1581).

The mezzanine floor houses the Loeser Collection of 14th-16th century paintings and sculptures, donated in 1928 by the American art critic Charles Loeser.

11. Galleria degli Uffizi

Piazzale degli Uffizi 6
Tel 055.2388651. Booking advisable: tel 055.294883 8.15am-6.50pm (the ticket office closes at 6.05pm); closed Mon. Ticket 6.50 €, EU citizens: aged 18-25 3.25 €, under 18s e over 65s free. Art book store inside

The Uffizi **(5)** (1560-80)

(5)

(1)

were built by Cosimo I, who wanted all government offices and law courts close at hand. They were designed by Vasari and completed by Bernardo Buontalenti and Alfonso Parigi. To make room for them, a great many houses were demolished, as well as the church of San Pietro in Scheraggio, part of whose nave can be seen inside the Uffizi (*temporarily closed*).

The loggia on the second floor was walled up as early as 1581 by Francesco I, to house the Medici collections: it is now the Uffizi Gallery, one of the most famous museums in the world. The rooms display an impressive array of masterpieces of 13th to 18th-century painting, arranged chronologically and according to schools. The hallways have splendidly decorated ceilings and have been refurbished in recent years so as to recreate as far as possible the appearance they had at the time of Francesco

Princes and collectors

Like all great princes, the Medici were also great collectors, mainly of paintings, but also of statues, small bronzes, gemstones, porcelain, weapons, curios, exotic objects, scientific instruments, depending on the taste of the age or their personal inclination. Cosimo il Vecchio was the first to start a collection of ancient marble statues, bronzes, gemstones and scientific instruments. Lorenzo il Magnifico had a real passion for vases made from rock crystal, onyx, jasper and other semiprecious stones. Cosimo I acquired objects from Africa and pre-Columbian America, and Etruscan bronzes as well. Cardinal Leopoldo, brother of Ferdinando II, started the collection of drawings, miniatures and self-portraits. Cosimo III had a liking for northern painters. Anna Maria Luisa loved figurines and trinkets of gold, ivory and gemstone. Almost all collected Roman statues and Roman copies of Greek originals. These various collections were housed on the top floor of the Uffizi, and were visible on request at least since 1591. In 1737 Anna Maria Luisa, the last member of the family, with the "Patto di famiglia" (Family Agreement) relinquished to the House of Lorraine all the treasures amassed by the Medici over the centuries, with the provision that they should remain in Florence and be accessible to the public. In 1771-72 the Grand Duke Peter Leopold began to break up the collections in accordance with the more scientific criteria of the age. The partitioning was completed in the late 19th century, and sections of the collections formed the core of the new museums, such as the Archaeological Museum, the Museo degli Argenti, the National Museum in the Bargello, the Museum of Anthropology and Ethnology, and later on the Museum of Science History, while the Uffizi Gallery became mainly a picture gallery **(2,3)**.

(3)

(2)

Via dei Georgofili

This narrow alley behind the Uffizi, whose existence was unknown even to many Florentines, became tragically famous on 27 May 1993, when a car bomb exploding shortly after 1am killed five people and ravaged the area. The famous Accademia dei Georgofili (Academy of Agriculture Lovers), founded in 1753, lost most of its ancient library, the Uffizi **(4)** also suffered substantial damage. Now everything has been rebuilt, in such a way as to distinguish clearly old and new parts, and the streets are busy once again, but that traumatic event remains etched in the collective memory of Florence.

(4)

I, with Roman busts, statues, sarcophagi, and portraits of famous people. A veritable jewel, for its decoration and for the works of art it contains, is the octagonal Tribune **(1)**, built by

Corridoio Vasariano

In 1565 Cosimo I directed Vasari to build a passageway that would enable him to go secretly from Palazzo Vecchio to the new ducal residence at Palazzo Pitti, passing through the Uffizi and over the Ponte Vecchio. A walk in the Vasari Corridor **(5)** offers some very unusual views, and allows a quick glimpse of the truly matchless collection of self-portraits belonging to the Uffizi, part of which is on display in the corridor. Unfortunately, only guided tours during limited periods of the year are admitted *(info and booking: tel 055.2654321)*.

(5)

Buontalenti for the collections' most precious objects, and used since the 18th century to display famous sculptures, such as the *Medici Venus*. At the end of the third hallway don't forget to step out on the terrace above the Loggia dei Lanzi for a stunning view of the square and of Palazzo Vecchio. And as you descend the Buontalenti staircase to the lower floor, where some rooms have now been opened, look up after the first landing and see the mark left by the window-frame hurled against the ceiling by the blast in Via dei Georgofili, on 27 May 1993.

12. Ponte Vecchio

The Old Bridge, with its jewellery shops projecting over the river **(6)**, is perhaps the monument most easily associated with Florence the world over. It is believed that a bridge existed on this site since Roman times. The present bridge was built in 1345 in place of a previous bridge that had been swept away by a flood, this was the only bridge to be spared by the retreating German army in 1944, at the expense of the ancient buildings at both ends of the bridge, which were razed to the ground.

Boating on the river

In summer one can glide down the Arno between Ponte alle Grazie and Ponte alla Carraia on traditional boats refurbished by the Society of "Renaioli" (the workers who in former times dredged the river bed). The tour lasts approx. 45 min, costs 11 € (5-14s 5 €) and must be booked by ringing 347.7982356 (www.renaioli.it).

(6)

THE QUARTER OF

*R*ound and round we go, ending up almost where we started. But along the way we will see marvellous sights, beginning with one of the most beautiful and important churches of Florence. Surely you did not think that

KEY

1. Piazza S. Croce
2. Basilica di S. Croce (Museo dell'Opera di Santa Croce)
3. Casa Buonarroti
4. Synagogue and Jewish Museum
5. S. Maria Maddalena de' Pazzi (Perugino *Crucifixion*)
6. Convento delle Oblate
7. Museo nazionale di antropologia ed etnologia
8. Badia fiorentina
9. Museo Nazionale del Bargello
10. Piazza S. Firenze (Oratory of St Filippo Neri)
11. Museo di Storia della Scienza

The National Museum, opened in 1865, displays 15th to 18th-century sculpture, with statues by Michelangelo, Cellini and others.

Museo del Bargello

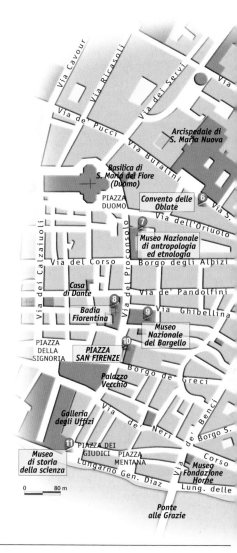

SANTA CROCE

just one itinerary would cover the entire centre of town, did you? Onward, then, through narrow streets squeezed between ancient palaces, and now and then across a vast square, full of light and history…

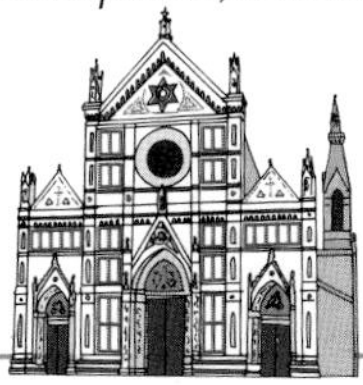

This great Franciscan church, begun in 1294 by Arnolfo di Cambio and completed about 1385, is famous also for its tombs and cenotaphs of famous Italians.

Basilica di Santa Croce

Via Laura
Via della Colonna
Pergola
Borgo Pinti
Alfani
PIAZZA M. D'AZEGLIO
5
S. Maria Maddalena de' Pazzi
Via Farini
Via dei Pilastri
4
Sinagoga e Museo Ebraico
Borgo Pinti
Via di Mezzo
Chiesa di S. Ambrogio
PIAZZA SALVEMINI
Via Pietrapiana
PIAZZA DEI CIOMPI
Via de' Pepi
Verdi
Allegri
PIAZZA GHIBERTI
Via dell'Agnolo
3
Casa Buonarroti
Via Ghibellina
Borgo
Via de' Macci
PIAZZA SANTA CROCE
1
2
Via di S. Giuseppe
delle Casine
Basilica di Santa Croce
Biblioteca Nazionale Centrale
Via Tripoli
PIAZZA DEI CAVALLEGGERI
Lung. della Zecca Vecchia
Fiume Arno

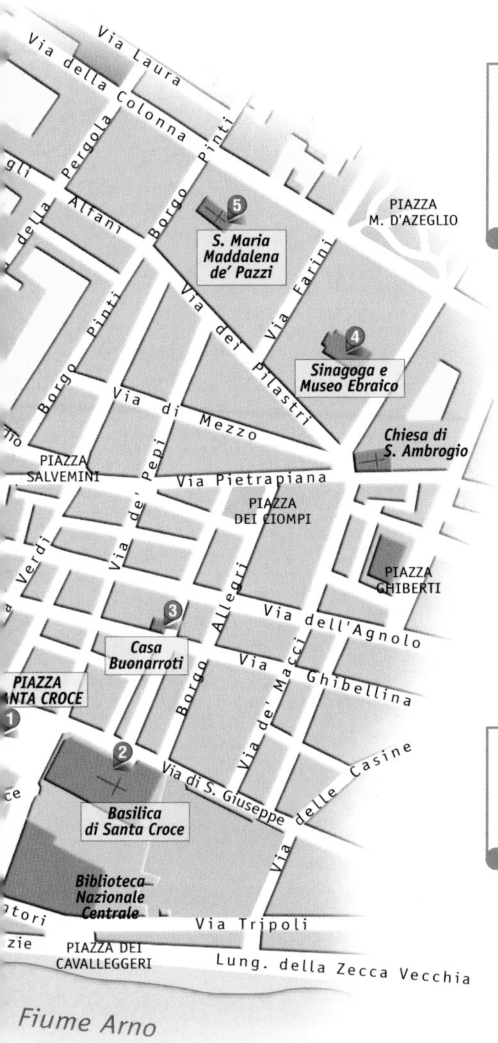

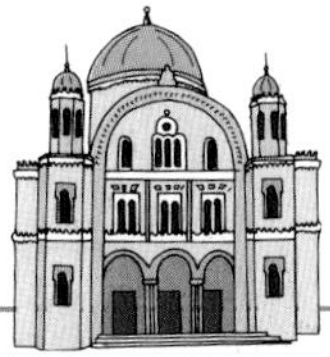

The building (1874-1882) reflects the eclectic taste of the age and has distinctive Moorish traits.

Sinagoga

1. Piazza Santa Croce

As paintings and prints testify, this was since the 14th century the venue for jousts, tournaments and games. In the 18th century the railing around the field was replaced by small columns and stone benches. On the south side of the piazza are picturesque buildings with projecting upper floors; the façade of the Palazzo dell'Antella is covered with frescoes (1619-20). Opposite the church is Palazzo Cocchi-Serristori (*c* 1470), possibly by Giuliano da Sangallo, flanked by Via Torta (crooked), built on the foundations of the Roman amphitheatre.

2. Basilica di Santa Croce and Museo dell'Opera di S. Croce

Piazza Santa Croce
Tel 055.2466105
Weekdays 9.30am-5.30pm;
Sun and holidays 1-5.30pm
Joint ticket 5 €, concessions
3 €; residents of the province
of Florence and under 11s free

The huge Franciscan church of the Holy Cross **(1)** was designed by Arnolfo di Cambio. Building began in 1294 and ended about 1385; the bell tower collapsed in 1514, the façade was never finished. Both were added in the 19th century: the façade by Niccolò Matas (1853-63), the tower by Gaetano Baccani (1847). The scowling Dante on the steps **(2)** also

(2)

(1)

A historic football game

In old times "livery" or "costume" football was played by young men from the most noble families: even the two future Medici popes, Leo X and Clement VII, were enthusiastic players. It then fell into disuse, the last official match taking place in 1739. A memorable match was played on 17 February 1530, while Florence was under siege. In 1930, when the game was revived, that remarkable event served as model. The four teams of 27 "calcianti" (kickers) each, represent the ancient quarters of Florence: S. Croce, S. Giovanni, S. Maria Novella, S. Spirito. Before the match, a colourful pageant winds through the town. The team that wins the tournament is awarded a white calf. The game, because of the brutality of its hand-to-hand fighting, resembles more rugby than soccer. After being moved several times – first to Piazza della Signoria (too risky for the statues), then to Boboli (too damaging for the plants) – the "Calcio in costume" has finally returned to Piazza S. Croce, its natural venue, as the marble plaques on nos. 7 and 21, marking the half-way line, prove beyond doubt. The tournament attracts tourist crowds, but the furious scuffles that sometimes erupt on the field or among supporters proclaim that this tradition is still very much alive with locals.

dates from that time. The austere interior has great 14th-century pictorial cycles. Observe the main chapel, with frescoes and stained glass windows by Agnolo Gaddi, and, to the right of it, the Peruzzi and Bardi chapels, with frescoes by Giotto (the *Scenes from the life of St Francis* (3), painted in 1320-25, are one of his masterpieces). Also of note are the pulpit by Benedetto da Maiano (1475), and the tabernacle with Donatello's *Annunciation* (1435).

From the cloister, damaged in 1966 (see the plaques marking the levels reached by the floods

Museo della Fondazione Horne

Via dei Benci 6, Tel 055.244661 9am-1pm; closed Sun and holidays. Ticket 5 €

The British scholar and collector Herbert Percy Horne bought this 15th century palace and had it refurbished under his direction in 1912-14. The museum displays his collection, with some great works of art, such as a Pietro Lorenzetti triptych, a Simone Martini diptych, a *St Stephen* attributed to Giotto, a *Crucifixion* by Filippino Lippi. Its most fascinating aspect, however, is that it re-creates, through furnishings, ceramics and objects of everyday use, the mansion of a Renaissance gentleman, and is at the same time an interesting example of a late 19th-century collector's taste.

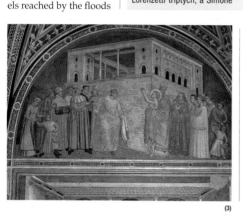

The entrance to the museum is between the first and the third cloister. On display are 14th and 15th-century detached frescoes, sinopias and paintings, and in the refectory the splendid Taddeo Gaddi frescoes (*Last Supper and Tree of the Cross*) and the great Cimabue Crucifix, symbol of the damage inflicted on the artistic heritage by the flood of 1966.

(3)

that have hit Florence), one enters the Cappella de' Pazzi (4), a late Brunelleschi masterpiece, decorated with Luca della Robbia medallions.

(4)

Burials and memorials

S. Croce owes its fame also to the tombs and cenotaphs of illustrious Italians. The main monuments, starting from the right aisle, are Michelangelo's tomb (1564), by Vasari; Dante Alighieri's cenotaph (5) (1829); the monument to the poet Vittorio Alfieri, by Antonio Canova (1810); the tomb of the humanist Leonardo Bruni, designed by Bernardo Rossellino (1444-45), that served as prototype to many Florentine tombs. The monument to Gioacchino Rossini dates from

(5)

1900, that to the poet Ugo Foscolo from 1939. Also of note, in the left transept, is the tomb of Countess Zamojska (although she is not an illustrious Italian), by Lorenzo Bartolini (1837-44). Going down the left aisle we find, opposite Bruni's, the monument to another humanist, Carlo Marsuppini, by Desiderio da Settignano (1454), then the monument to 19th-century politician Vittorio Fossombroni, also by Bartolini, Lorenzo Ghiberti's tomb, and finally Galileo's.

3. Museo della Casa Buonarroti

Via Ghibellina 70
Tel 055.241752
9.30am-2pm; closed Tue
Ticket 6.50 €, concessions 4 €

The house was bought by Michelangelo in 1508, enlarged after 1612 by Michelangelo the Younger, further enriched by other descendants, and bequeathed to the town by Cosimo Buonarroti in 1858. Besides displaying early masterpieces by Michelangelo **(1)**, it is a fascinating tribute to a family that had several remarkable members besides their famous forebear. In the course of time, collections of painting, sculpture, ceramics, archaeological items were added to Michelangelo's works. The museum boasts the largest collection in the world of Michelangelo drawings. They are displayed in rotation in a special room.

4. Synagogue and Jewish Museum

Via Farini 4, tel 055.245252
Nov-Mar: Sun-Thu 10am-3pm, Fri. 10am-2pm; Apr-May and Sep-Oct: Sun-Thu 10am-5pm, Fri 10am-2pm; Jun-Aug: Sun-Thu 10am-6pm, Fri 10am-2pm; closed Sat
Joint ticket 4 €, concessions 3 €

When the centre of Florence with the former Ghetto was demolished, it became necessary to build a new synagogue **(2)**. Designed by Marco Treves, Mariano Falcini and Vincenzo Micheli, the building (1874-1882) reflects the eclectic taste

(2)

of the times, and is clearly influenced by the Moorish Revival. The interior is decorated with frescoes, wood carvings, mosaics and stained glass windows. The attached Jewish Museum traces the history of Jews in Florence and displays precious textiles, silver vessels, ancient ritual objects.

5. S. Maria Maddalena de' Pazzi Perugino Crucifixion

Borgo Pinti 58
Tel 055.2478420
Weekdays 9am-noon, 5-5.20pm and 6-7pm, holidays 9-10.45am and 5-6.30pm; Entrance free, donation advised

Founded in 1257, the church was re-

(1)

S. Maria Nuova

Piazza di S. Maria Nuova
Florence's oldest hospital **(3)** was founded in 1288 by Folco Portinari, father of Dante's Beatrice, and much enlarged over the centuries. Traces of Portinari's tomb are in the church of S. Egidio, at the centre of the portico by Buontalenti; in the cloister to the left of the church is the gravestone of Monna Tessa (Mistress Theresa), whose engagement in nursing the sick is said to have persuaded Portinari to found the hospital.

(3)

built in 1479-1500 by Giuliano da Sangallo, who also designed the cloister. The paintings date mostly from the 17th-18th century, and

(4)

the main chapel is a rare instance of Roman Baroque in Florence. Its most prized possession is a masterpiece by Perugino, the fresco of the *Crucifixion* (1493-96) **(4)**, in the former chapter house.

6. Convento delle Oblate

Via S. Egidio 21-23

The former convent opposite the hospital, until 1936 home to the nuns who nursed the sick, houses two tiny museums, the Prehistory Museum and the History and Topography Museum "Firenze com'era" (Florence as it used to be). No. 23 was until 1660 the women's ward.

Museo di Preistoria Paolo Graziosi

Via Sant'Egidio 21
Tel 055.295159
9.30am-12.30pm, (Tue and Thu until 4.30pm), closed Sun and holidays; ticket 3 €
The museum, founded in 1946 by Paolo Graziosi, a local palaeontologist, boasts the skeleton of a cave bear found in the north of Tuscany; also on display are relics from the Upper Paleolithic and later periods, and photographs of rock paintings.

7. Museo nazionale di antropologia ed etnologia

Via del Proconsolo 12
Tel 055.2396449
9am-1pm (Sat until 5pm); closed Wed
Ticket 4 €, concessions 2 €; joint ticket for all science museums available

The National Museum of Anthropology and Ethnology, founded in 1869, is highly regarded among scholars and interested amateurs, but sadly neglected by the general public. Admittedly, it does little to attract visitors, and practically hides the (few) panels that should help them find their bearings among the profuse collections of pottery, textiles, jewels and weapons documenting the cultures of non-European peoples, gathered by expeditions in the 19th and early 20th century **(5)**. Thrilling exhibits are the relics of James Cook's last voyage to the Pacific (1776-79), acquired by Peter Leopold, and the Medici collections, with a rare Brazilian feather cloak bought by Cosimo II in 1618.

(5)

Museo Storico Topografico "Firenze com'era"

Via dell'Oriolo 24
Tel 055.2768224
Mon-Tue 9am-2pm, Sat 9am-7pm; Oct to May also Wed 9am-2pm. Ticket 2.70 € (18-25s and over 65s: 2 €; 3-17s: 1 €; under 3s free)
This small, well ordered museum traces the

(6)

history of Florence **(6)** from Stone Age settlement to 19th-century town, through relief maps, archaeological remains, prints and paintings. Famous exhibits are the reproduction of the *Pianta della Catena* (Chain Map, 1470), the *Lunettes* by Iustus van Utens (1599) depicting the Medici villas, the Zocchi prints, documenting the 18th-century town, the images and the relief map of the Mercato Vecchio and the Jewish Ghetto before demolition.

Casa di Dante

Via Santa Margherita 1, tel 055.219416; Tue-Sat 10am-5pm, Sun 10am-1pm, closed Mon and last Sun in the month; ticket 4 €

The house "where Dante was born" **(1)** is, to put it bluntly, a fake: a fanciful 1910 reconstruction, on the site where the houses of the Alighieri are believed to have stood. Nearby "Dante's Church" (San-

ta Margherita de' Cerchi) is a guess: perhaps this is where Dante wedded Gemma Donati. Anyhow, it was the church attended by the Portinari, whose houses were close by, in the present Via del Corso.

(1)

8. Badia fiorentina

Entrance also from Via Dante Alighieri 1, open to visitors only Mon after 3pm

Only the apse remains of the church built by Arnolfo di Cambio on the site of an abbey founded in 978: its windows can be seen from Via del Proconsolo, next to a portal by Benedetto da Rovezzano **(2)** (1495). The hexagonal bell tower (1310-30) is one of the landmarks of Florence. The church was radically altered in the 17th

(2)

century, even its axis was turned around. Small wonder the interior lacks stylistic unity. It has however some fine

work by Mino da Fiesole (a bas-relief and two tombs, dating from 1464-81) and a panel painting by Filippino Lippi (*c* 1480). The Chiostro degli Aranci, by Bernardo Rossellino, with frescoes depicting Scenes from the *Life of St Benedict*, is a fine example of early Renaissance architecture.

9. Museo Nazionale del Bargello

Via del Proconsolo 4
Tel 055.2388606.
8.15am-1.50pm; closed 2nd and 4th Mon, 1st, 3rd and 5th Sun of the month; last ticket sold at 13.20. Ticket 4 €, concessions 2 €; 7 € when there are temporary exhibits

The massive Palazzo del Capitano del Popolo **(3)** was built in 1255-1261, incorporating an older tower, and was enlarged several times. The magnificent courtyard dates from *c* 1295, the staircase is by Neri di Fioravanti (1345-67). From 1574 on the palace was home to

(3)

the Capitano di giustizia, also called "Bargello", i.e. the chief of police. Part of the palace was used as jail, and much altered. The alterations were removed during the 19th-century renovation. The National Museum opened in 1865. It displays 14th to 18th-century sculpture, by Michelangelo, Cellini, Sansovino, Giambologna, also by Donatello **(4)** and two of his disciples, Desiderio da Settignano and Antonio Rossellino. There is also a fine collection of busts by Verrocchio, Antonio del Pollaiolo and Mino da Fiesole, and many works by the Della Robbia family. Also of note are the pottery, the small bronzes that belonged to the Medici, the Carrand collection (jewellery, enamels and small paintings). A special mention is due to the truly unique ivories.

(4)

10. Piazza S. Firenze

S. Firenze (1645-1775), former convent of the Oratorian Fathers, is a fine example of late Baroque, quite rare in Florence. It is now a law court, the oratory is used as courtroom and can be seen only during hearings. The Church of S. Filippo Neri, on the left, is still used for worship, and has a fine coffered ceiling (1715). Opposite is Palazzo Gondi, designed by Giuliano da Sangallo (1490), with a beautiful courtyard (*closed to the public*).

11. Museo di Storia della Scienza

Piazza dei Giudici 1
Tel 055.265311
9.30am-5pm (Tue and Sat 9.30am-1pm); closed Sun and holidays (except 2nd Sun of the month in Oct-May, 10am-1pm). Ticket 6.50 €

The History of Science Museum, one of the town's main museums **(5)**, is based on the Medici and Lorraine collections. On display are astrolabes, clocks, mathematical instruments, an Arab celestial globe, one of the oldest calculating machines (1625-1695), a 16th-century armillary sphere. The most treasured instruments are those that belonged to Galileo: two telescopes, a compass, the objective lens he used to observe Jupiter's moons, and more. Among the relics, the middle finger of his right hand, detached when the body was moved to S. Croce in 1737.

(5)

29

THE "OLTRARNO"

*"*O*ltrarno" or "Diladdarno" (beyond the Arno), as Florentines say, is the part of town across the river from the old city centre. San Niccolò, Santo Spirito, San Frediano – neighbourhoods where streets, squares, shops and workshops (the "botteghe") still maintain a genuine,*

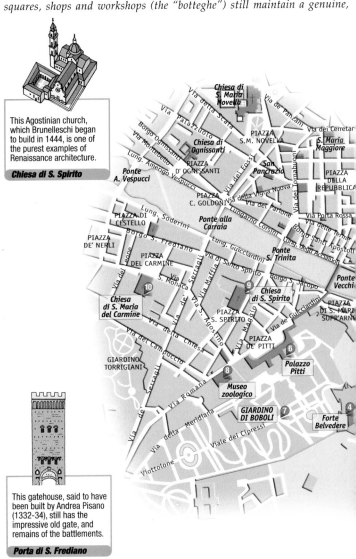

This Agostinian church, which Brunelleschi began to build in 1444, is one of the purest examples of Renaissance architecture.

Chiesa di S. Spirito

This gatehouse, said to have been built by Andrea Pisano (1332-34), still has the impressive old gate, and remains of the battlements.

Porta di S. Frediano

old-time Florentine feel. Piazza S. Spirito, filled with happy crowds on summer evenings, is an oasis of peace in daytime, quite different from the busy town centre. From the hills, Piazzale Michelangelo and Forte Belvedere, offer stunning views of the town.

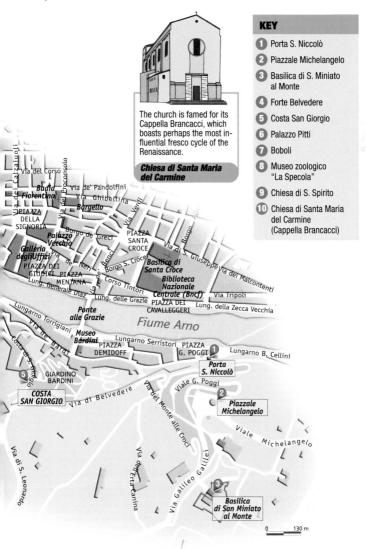

The church is famed for its Cappella Brancacci, which boasts perhaps the most influential fresco cycle of the Renaissance.

Chiesa di Santa Maria del Carmine

KEY

1. Porta S. Niccolò
2. Piazzale Michelangelo
3. Basilica di S. Miniato al Monte
4. Forte Belvedere
5. Costa San Giorgio
6. Palazzo Pitti
7. Boboli
8. Museo zoologico "La Specola"
9. Chiesa di S. Spirito
10. Chiesa di Santa Maria del Carmine (Cappella Brancacci)

0   130 m

lane leads to the Giardino dell'Iris, dedicated to the flower that is the symbol of Florence, over 1500 varieties of which can be seen in full bloom in May (*tel 055.483112 for info on opening days of the Iris Garden, entrance free*).

3. Basilica di San Miniato al Monte

Via Monte alle Croci
Tel 055.2342731
Summer: 8.30am-7pm;
Winter: 8am-12.30pm and
2.30pm-7pm. Entrance free

The 11th to13th-century St Minias on the Mountain (4), a masterpiece of Romanesque architec-

1. Porta San Niccolò

St Nicholas Gate (1), the only gateway to have kept its original height, rises at the centre of the square named after the architect and urban planner Giuseppe Poggi. Ramps lead from the square to Piazzale Michelangelo, which can also be reached by car or by bus (no. 13), by way of the scenic Viale Michelangelo.

2. Piazzale Michelangelo

This vast terrace (2) designed by Poggi, called simply "i' ppiazzale" by Florentines, who flock here on summer

evenings, offers a well-known panorama of the city. At the centre is a questionable monument to Michelangelo, with bronze copies of several of his statues. A short

Casa-museo Rodolfo Siviero

Lungarno Serristori 3
Tel 055.2345219. Sun and Mon 10am-1pm, Sat. 10am-6pm (summer 9.30am-12.30pm/4.30-7.30pm), entrance free
In the small villa where he lived until his death in 1983, one can visit the private collection of Rodolfo Siviero (3), from Etruscan relics to 20th-century paintings. The visit gives an insight into the taste of this personage – secret agent, Minister Plenipotentiary, art expert – best known for having tracked down many works of art looted by Nazis during the war.

ture, rises atop the hill. The geometrically patterned marble façade frames a 13th-century mosaic. The interior has a raised presbytery over a crypt decorated with Taddeo Gaddi frescoes; the nave has a patterned floor (1207), and leads up to a freestanding chapel by Michelozzo (1448). From the sacristy (1387), frescoed by

(4)

Raccolta
"A. Della Ragione"

Temporarily in the villa inside Forte Belvedere; for info ring 055.2001256.

The collection comprises about 250 works of art, donated in 1970 by Alberto Della Ragione to the municipality, and illustrating 20th-century artistic movements in Italy up to the 1960s, with works by De Chirico, De Pisis, Guttuso and many more. It can be visited when the Forte is open.

Spinello Aretino, one enters the cloister, with fragments of Paolo Uccello frescoes. To the left of the church is the cemetery "delle Porte Sante" (*c* 1860), with grand Neo-Gothic and Neo-Renaissance tombs.

4. Forte Belvedere (or di San Giorgio)

Via San Leonardo
Tel 055.2342822 - winter noon-5pm; summer 2-7pm; closed Mon

St George's Fort can be reached from San Miniato by walk (*or by taxi: driving there by car is not advisable*), going down Via del Monte alle Croci and turning into the steep Via di Belvedere, which from the small Porta S. Miniato skirts a section of the old city wall. Turning instead into Via dell'Erta Canina, one will discover a stretch of countryside literally "at the doorstep" of Florence. Designed by Buontalenti in 1590-95, the Fort (5), that has at its centre an older villa, offers spectacular views of the town. It is used as venue for temporary exhibitions, particularly those involving large sculptures: the bastions are an ideal setting.

5. Costa San Giorgio

From the 13th-century Porta S. Giorgio one can descend towards the Ponte Vecchio by steep, picturesque Costa San Giorgio. A plaque on the wall of no. 19 marks Galileo's house.

Museo and Giardino Bardini

Museo Bardini
Piazza de' Mozzi 1
Tel 055.2342427,
temporarily closed
In a 13th-century *palazzo*, much altered in the late 19th century, the museum established by the antiques dealer Stefano Bardini and donated to the municipality in 1922 displays furniture, tapestries, weapons, paintings and sculptures, from antiquity to Baroque times.

Giardino Bardini
Via dei Bardi 1/r
Tel 055.294883,
8.15am-dusk; closed 1st and last Mon of the month.
Ticket 8 €, concessions 4 € (joint ticket with Galleria del Costume, Argenti, Porcellane and Boboli Gardens)
This vast garden, full of ancient relics, and situated in the heart of Florence, was once owned by Stefano Bardini, who embellished it with statues from his collection. From the loggia one enjoys a unique panorama.

(5)

Chiesa di Santa Felicita

The Romanesque church of St Felicitas, in the small square by the same name, was entirely redone in the 16th century. It was used as chapel by the Lorraine Grand Dukes, who would watch Mass from the Vasari Corridor **(1)**, which runs over the portico. There are two Pontormo masterpieces: the *Deposition* (1528) and the *Annunciation* (1525).

(3)

6. Palazzo Pitti

The grand *palazzo* **(2)**, commonly credited to Brunelleschi (although he died in 1446), was built for the Pitti family *c* 1458. The Medici bought it in 1549 and turned it into a princely mansion. It was enlarged by Ammannati, who designed the great court, and again in the 17th century; in 1765 and 1839 two perpendicular wings were added at each end. Having been the abode of the Medici, of the Lorraine, and lastly of the Italian royal family, the Savoy, the palace is today home to some outstanding museums.

7. Giardino di Boboli

Piazza Pitti - Tel 055.2651838 8.15am-dusk; closed 1st and last Mon of the month; ticket 8 €, concessions 4 € (joint ticket with Galleria del Costume, Argenti, Porcellane and Giardino Bardini in Via dei Bardi)

Designed *c* 1550 by Niccolò Pericoli, called Tribolo, the Boboli Gardens were completed by Ammannati and others, and are a splendid example of formal Italian park. The

(4)

highlights are Buontalenti's *Grotta Grande* (1583-1586; *guided tours every hour: after 11.30am meeting point in front of the grotto*), the 17th-century amphitheatre, and Neptune's Fountain **(3)** (1565). On the upper slopes are the *Giardino del Cavaliere* and the *Casino del Cavaliere* (Chevalier's Garden and Lodge), built in 1700 for Gian Gastone de' Medici. The central avenue, called

(2)

The museums in Pitti Palace

For telephone bookings ring 055.294883
Unless there is a temporary exhibition, a joint ticket for all museums is available.

Galleria Palatina

Tel 055.2388614; 8.15am-6.50pm, closed Mon. Ticket: 8.50 €, concessions 4.25 € (joint ticket with Royal Apartments and Gallery of Modern Art)
Opened to the public by Leopold of Lorraine in 1828 and housed in the former grand-ducal apartments, in rooms superbly decorated with frescoes by Pietro da Cortona and Volterrano, the Palatine Gallery maintains the feel of a private collection, with paintings hung according to taste, not scholarly criteria. There are works by Titian and Raphael (such as the *Woman with the Veil*, and the *Madonna della Seggiola*) **(5)**, also by Perugino, Tintoretto, Filippo Lippi, Andrea del Sarto, Caravaggio, Guido Reni, and by non-Italian painters, such as Rubens, Van Dyck and Velásquez.
The lavish Royal Apartments (closed in January) have decorations and furnishings dating from the Medici, Lorraine and Savoy eras, i.e. from the 16th to the 19th century.

Museo degli Argenti

Tel 055.2388709-761
Opening times and tickets s. Boboli Gardens
The Silver Museum, in the splendidly decorated former summer apartments of the Grand Duke, displays a great variety of precious objects **(6)**, that testify to the taste of their princely collectors. Of great interest are the onyx and gemstone vases that belonged to Lorenzo il Magnifico, the German ivories of Prince Matthias de' Medici, the jewels and trinkets of Anna Maria Luisa de' Medici; also the cameos, the Chinese and Japanese porcelain, and the exotic collections, indicating the interest of the Medici for far-away lands.

Galleria d'Arte Moderna

Tel 055.2388616
Opening times and tickets s. Palatine Gallery
On display in the second-floor rooms, that were used by the royal family until 1920, are masterpieces of 19th and early 20th-century Italian and Tuscan painting and sculpture. The historical paintings depict events and passions of the period leading up to Italian Unification.
The gallery also owns a remarkable collection of Macchiaioli, with very important paintings by Giovanni Fattori and by Telemaco Signorini.

Galleria del Costume

Tel 055.2388713; opening times and tickets s. Boboli Gardens
The Costume Gallery in the Palazzina della Meridiana (1778-1840) displays clothes and accessories illustrating the history of fashion from the 18th to the 20th century.

Museo delle Carrozze

Temporarily closed, can be visited on request: tel 055.2388611
Several grand carriages from the Lorraine and Savoy period are housed in the palace's right wing; sadly, no opening of the museum is in sight.

Museo delle Porcellane

Boboli Gardens
Tel 055.2388709
Opening times and tickets s. Boboli Gardens
The Porcelain Museum is a gem immersed in the green of Boboli: located in the secluded Chevalier's Lodge, in rooms with delicate 18th century decorations, it displays exquisite porcelain objects that have belonged to three dynasties. Of particular note are the figurines representing Neapolitan folk costumes, the service given by Napoleon to his sister Elisa, the services and figurines made by the Manifattura di Doccia, founded near Florence in 1735.

"Viottolone", flanked by statues **(4)**, leads to the Piazzale dell'Isolotto, with a large basin and Giambologna's Fountain of Oceanus. From the Lorraine period date the *Kaffeehaus* (1774-76), high up in the park, which boasts a fine view, the *Prato delle Colonne* (1776) and the *Limonaia* (1785). The park was opened to the public in 1776 by the Grand Duke Peter Leopold. One exit is opposite the entrance to Forte Belvedere: from there one can reach the Giardino Bardini.

8. Museo di Storia Naturale - Sezione zoologica "La Specola"

Via Romana 17
Tel 055.2288251
9am-1pm (Skeleton Room: Tue, Thu and Sun 9am-1pm), Sat to 5pm; closed Wed and main holidays; ticket 4 €, concessions 2 €; joint ticket with all science museums available

(1)

Founded by Peter Leopold and opened to the public in 1775, the Natural History Museum **(1)** has one of the largest zoological collections of Italy. Its main attraction, however, are the 1400 anatomical wax models, the largest collection in the world of its kind, made for teaching purposes between 1771 and 1893 by the Officina di ceroplastica (Wax Modelling Workshop). The most famous is the *Recumbent statue illustrating the superficial lymphatic system*, commonly called "lo Spellato" (the Skinned Man), as it portrays a body without the skin.

9. Chiesa di Santo Spirito

Piazza S. Spirito - Tel 055.210030 10am-noon/4-6pm; closed Wed afternoon, Sun morning and holidays. Entrance free

Cenacoli

Besides the ones named in the itineraries, there are other fine "Cenacoli", i.e. frescoes in refectories depicting the Last Supper. The Cenacolo di Andrea del Sarto, in the former convent of San Salvi (*Via S. Salvi 16, tel 055.2388603, open 8.30am-1.50pm; closed Mon, entrance free*), was painted by the artist in 1511-1527, and is considered his masterpiece **(3)**. The adjoin-

(3)

ing rooms house a small collection of panel paintings and altarpieces. The Cenacolo di Santa Apollonia (*via XXVII Aprile 1, tel 055.2388607, 8.30am-1.50pm; closed 1st, 3rd and 5th Sun of the month, 2nd and 4th Mon of the month; entrance free*), in the former Benedictine nunnery founded in 1339, is dedicated to the art of Andrea del Castagno, killed by the plague in 1457. Another *Last Supper*, attributed to Perugino and assistants, is in the refectory of another former nunnery (*Cenacolo di Fuligno, via Faenza, 40/42, tel 055.2386982, Mon, Tue and Sat 9am-noon, donation advised*).

Cenacolo di Santo Spirito (Fondazione Romano)
Piazza S. Spirito 29
Tel 055.287043
Sat 10.30am-1.30pm; ticket 2.20 €, concessions 1.70 €

The Agostinian Church of the Holy Spirit (2), begun by Brunelleschi in 1444 and completed by others, is one of the purest examples of Renaissance architecture. The interior has 40 semicircular chapels, a few of which retain the original altarpiece. Among the

most remarkable is the Corbinelli Chapel, an early work by Sansovino

Via Maggio

In Florence there is certainly no lack of Renaissance *palazzi*, but Via Maggio can boast a truly remarkable number of them: see at no. 26 the palace of Bianca Cappello, mistress and then wife to Francesco I, with fine 16th-century *graffiti* and a portal by Buontalenti (1572); at no. 13 Palazzo Ridolfi, by Santi di Tito; at no. 7 Palazzo Ricasoli-Firidolfi; at no. 37 the house of Bernardo Buontalenti. No. 8 is Casa Guidi **(4)**, where Elisabeth Barrett Browning lived and died (1861) (*Apr-Nov: Mon, Wed, Fri 3-6pm; donation advised*).

(4)

(2)

(5)

(1492). From the left aisle one enters a vestibule with a coffered vault and an octagonal sacristy, both by Giuliano da Sangallo (1489-94). To the left of the church is the Cenacolo (refectory), home to a *Crucifixion* and to fragments of a *Last Supper*, both attributed to Orcagna. Also displayed is the splendid collection of sculptures donated by the antique dealer Salvatore Romano, including a Madonna and Child by Jacopo della Quercia.

10. Chiesa di Santa Maria del Carmine

7.30am-noon and 5-6.30pm (except during Mass), Entrance free
Cappella Brancacci
*Piazza del Carmine 14
Tel 055.2382195
10am-4.30pm, Sun 1-4.30pm; closed Tue and main holidays; booking required (tel 055.2768224/055.2768558 every day 9am-1pm and 2-7pm, or by applying directly at the entrance, to the right of the façade)
Tickets 4 or 6 €, concessions 3 or 5 €, children 1.50 or 2.50 € (joint tickets with Palazzo Vecchio 8, 6 and 3 € respectively, valid 3 months);*

family tickets available Includes a 40 min video, shown in the refectory before the visit to the chapel.

The church, founded in the 13th century, but almost entirely rebuilt after it was gutted by fire in 1771, owes its fame to the frescoes in the Cappella Brancacci, possibly the most influential pictorial cycle of the entire Renaissance. The superb frescoes **(5, 6)**, that have regained the original delicate colours due to extensive restoration in the 1980s, were painted by Masolino and Masaccio in 1424-1427. Left unfinished when Masaccio left for Rome (where he died at the age of 27), they were completed after 1480 by Filippino Lippi. They include some absolute masterpieces, such as the *Expulsion from the Garden of Eden* and *The Tribute Money*, both by Masaccio. Across the nave, creating a strange contrast, opens the Cappella Corsini, a singular instance of exuberant Roman Baroque in Florence.

(6)

The quarter of San Frediano

The San Frediano Gatehouse, said to have been built by Andrea Pisano (1332-34), retains the ancient gate and part of the battlements. It is surrounded by a fairly "uncontaminated" working-class Florence, with modest buildings and small shops and workshops. Factory workers and artisans have lived here since the Middle Ages: street names, such as Via dei Tessitori (weavers), Via dei Cardatori (carders), Piazza del Tiratoio (where wool was hung out to dry after washing and dyeing) remind us that this is where the all-important woollen cloth was made. Of all the quarters of Florence, San Frediano **(7)** is the one that has remained most true to its origins, and that is why the term "sanfredianino" (inhabitant of San Frediano) still carries a distinctive flavour in the local idiom.

THE MEDICI AND

he last itinerary focuses on the Medici and "their" Florence: their church, their palace, the monastery of which they were patrons, the museums they founded or that originated from their collections. A fascinating voyage in time, side by side with Cosimo, Piero, Lorenzo and Giuliano,

Only the bell tower survives of the 13th-century church; the interior has many fine works of art.

Chiesa di Ognissanti

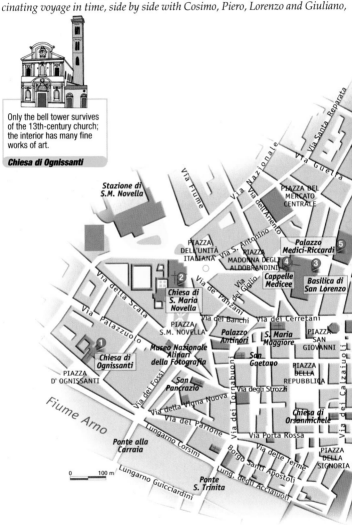

"THEIR" FLORENCE

that will take us from busy San Lorenzo – where they lived –, to Piazza San Marco, surrounded by museums, and to Piazza SS. Annunziata, beloved by Florentines but often ignored by tourist itineraries.

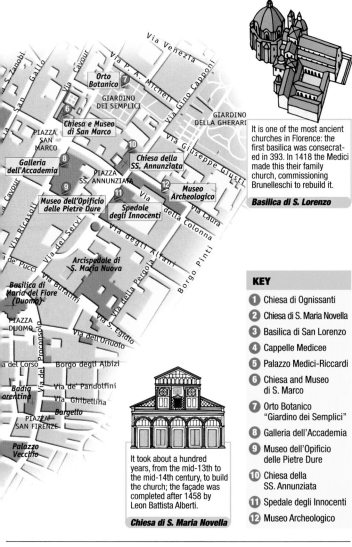

It is one of the most ancient churches in Florence: the first basilica was consecrated in 393. In 1418 the Medici made this their family church, commissioning Brunelleschi to rebuild it.

Basilica di S. Lorenzo

It took about a hundred years, from the mid-13th to the mid-14th century, to build the church; the façade was completed after 1458 by Leon Battista Alberti.

Chiesa di S. Maria Novella

KEY

1. Chiesa di Ognissanti
2. Chiesa di S. Maria Novella
3. Basilica di San Lorenzo
4. Cappelle Medicee
5. Palazzo Medici-Riccardi
6. Chiesa and Museo di S. Marco
7. Orto Botanico "Giardino dei Semplici"
8. Galleria dell'Accademia
9. Museo dell'Opificio delle Pietre Dure
10. Chiesa della SS. Annunziata
11. Spedale degli Innocenti
12. Museo Archeologico

1. Chiesa di Ognissanti

Borgo Ognissanti 42
Open weekdays 8am-noon/
4-7pm, holidays 4-6pm

(1)

Cascine

In the west of Florence, on the Arno, are the "Cascine". They owe their name (farmsteads) to a former Medici farm, made into a park and opened to the public in the early 19th century. The park, very crowded on sunny days, has shady avenues and many sports facilities, including a racecourse. At the entrance is the equestrian statue of King Victor Emanuel II, formerly in Piazza della Repubblica (then Piazza Vittorio Emanuele). At the other end, on the Piazzaletto dell'Indiano, is a small funeral monument (1874) to the Maharaja of Kolepoor, who died aged twenty in Florence in 1870 and was cremated at the confluence of the Mugnone and the Arno.

The Church of All Saints **(1)** was much altered in the 17th-18th century (the façade is by Bartolomeo Nigetti, 1637); only the bell tower survives from the 13th-century building. The interior has fine works of art, such as Botticelli's *St Augustine in his Study*, and, opposite, Ghirlandaio's *St Jerome*. To the left of the church are the cloister and the refectory, with a *Last Supper*, also by Ghirlandaio (*Open Mon, Tue and Sat 9am-noon; entrance free*).

2. Chiesa di S. Maria Novella

Piazza S. M. Novella
Tel 055.219257, 9.30am-5pm,
Fri and holidays 1-5pm
Tickets 2.50 €, concessions
1.50 € (under 11s and residents free)
__Museum:__ tel 055.282187;
9am-5pm, Sun 9am-2pm,
closed Fri. Tickets 2.70 €, concessions 2 €, children 1 €,
under 3s free. Last ticket sold
30 min before closing.

It took about a hundred years, from the mid-13th to the mid-14th century,

Museo Marino Marini

Piazza S. Pancrazio
Tel 055.219432
10am-5pm, closed Tue, Sun
and holidays (also Sat in May-
Sep); ticket 4 € 00
Set in the striking ambience of the former church of St Pancrace, the museum displays a large number of sculptures **(3)**, donated to Florence by Marino Marini (1901-1980), one of the greatest Italian sculptors of 20th century. The collection traces his artistic career through almost 200 works. The statues are placed on different levels and lit by natural light, thus creating a great (3) harmony between the building and the works of art.

for St Mary "the New" to be built; the façade **(2)** was completed after 1458 by Leon Battista Alberti, who designed the portal and the upper part. The interior has a

(2)

store of works of art, such as Giotto's *Crucifix* **(4)**, and the stunning fresco by Masaccio depicting the *Holy Trinity* (*c* 1427). The main chapel has frescoes by Ghirlandaio (1485-90), the elevated Strozzi Chapel Nardo di Cione frescoes inspired by Dante's *Divine Comedy*.

The entrance to the cloisters and the museum is from the square. From the Green Cloister, which owes its name to the greenish tint of its frescoes with scenes from Genesis (including Paolo Uccello's *The Flood* and *The Drunkenness of Noah*), one enters the Cappellone degli Spagnoli (Spanish Chapel), covered with frescoes (1366-68). The museum displays sacred vessels and embroidered textiles.

In nearby Via della Scala, at no. 16, is the ancient Officina Profumo-Farmaceutica, which until 1866 belonged to the friars of S. Maria Novella (s. chapter on *Shopping*).

S. Maria Novella Station

(5)

Florence has few contemporary buildings of note, but the Central Station, built in 1933-1935 by a group of Tuscan architects led by Giovanni Michelucci, is a fine specimen of Rationalist architecture **(5)**. Behind it, the Fortress of St John the Baptist, commonly called "Fortezza da Basso" (Lower Fortress) by Antonio da Sangallo (1534-35).

was consecrated as far back as 393 AD. In 1418 the Medici chose it as their family church, commissioning Brunelleschi to rebuild it. The façade was left unfinished **(6)**; Michelangelo later designed one, but it remained unbuilt. The interior is a great example of Renaissance architecture. Highlights are Desiderio da Settignano's Altar of the Sacrament (*c* 1460), the two Donatello pulpits

Museo Nazionale Alinari della Fotografia

Piazza Santa Maria Novella 14a/r, tel 055.216310 9.30am-7.30pm, Sat until 11.30pm, closed Wed. Tickets 9 €, concessions 7.50 €/6 €, under 5s free (last ticket sold 30 min before closing

The museum traces the history of photography by means of vintage material from the rich Alinari Archives (the Alinari brothers established a highly successful studio in Florence in 1852) and other sources. Also on display are works of great photographers past and present.

3. Basilica di San Lorenzo

Piazza S. Lorenzo Tel 055.216634 10am-5pm; closed Sun Ticket 2.50 €

This is one of the most ancient churches in Florence: the first basilica

(4)

(6)

Places to reach by bus

Museo Stibbert

*Via F. Stibbert 26
Tel 055.475520; Mon-Wed 10am-2pm, Fri-Sun 10am-6pm, closed Thu; ticket 5 €, concessions 2 €. Bus no. 4 from the Station, stop: Fabroni 3*

Created by the English financier and collector Frederick Stibbert (1838-1906) in his villa in the north of Florence, this is a rare example of 19th-century museum. Stibbert had the villa refurbished by the best architects and artisans of the time, and each room was meant to evoke the atmosphere of the countries and periods from which the exhibits came. The collections include weapons, costumes, furniture, tapestry, ceramics and paintings from the 16th to the 19th century. Most spectacular is the Cavalcade Room, with twelve life-size horsemen wearing European and Oriental armour dating from 1510-1630. The villa is surrounded by a fine English-style park with a pond, two small temples and a remarkable Orangerie.

Fiesole (1)

Bus no. 7 from the Station or from Piazza San Marco.
One can also get off the bus at San Domenico and walk the rest of the way, reaching Fiesole by the picturesque (but narrow and steep) *Via Vecchia Fiesolana* Fiesole, founded by Etruscans, and conquered by the Romans in

(1)

the 1st century BC, has many relics of the past. In the main square are the cathedral of St Romolus and the ancient St James's Chapel in the Archbishop's palace, behind the cathedral the Bandini Museum, the archaeological area, with the Roman theatre (still in use in the summer), remains of Roman baths, temples and an Etruscan wall, and a fine archaeological museum (*Via Portigiani, 27, tel 055.59118-59416; open summer 9.30am-7pm; winter 9.30am -5pm, closed Tue; St James's Chapel open only Sat and holidays 10am-7pm; joint ticket for: Area archeologica, Museo archeologico, Museo Bandini, Cappella di S. Jacopo 6.50 €, concessions 4.50 €, families 14.50 €).* A steep road leads to the Early Christian basilica of St Alexander and to the top of the hill. Here one can visit the 14th-century church and monastery of St Francis, with some ancient cells and a small museum displaying various items

collected by missionaries, mainly in China and Egypt.

Certosa (2)

Tel 055.2049226, open: Tue-Sat 9.15-11.30am/3-5pm (4.15pm in winter), Sun 3-5pm (4.15 in winter), closed Mon. Buses nos. 36-37 from the Station

Another short excursion, this time south of Florence, to a suburb called Galluzzo, takes us to the Certosa, a Carthusian monastery founded in 1342 by Niccolò Acciaioli and since 1958 inhabited by Cistercian monks. Surrounded by walls like a fortress, the monastery comprises several buildings and was altered repeatedly during the centuries.

(2)

(1460, with parts added in the 17th century), and the cantorial pulpit (1443), also by Donatello. From the left aisle one enters the Old Sacristy, conceived by Brunelleschi as a cube topped by a hemisphere (1420-28), with a bust of St Lawrence, attributed to Donatello, and the sarcophagus of Giovanni and

Piero de' Medici, uncle and father of Lorenzo il Magnifico, by Verrocchio (1472). Through the first cloister one enters the Biblioteca mediceo-laurenziana (*tel 055.210760, 9.30am-1.30pm, closed Mon and main holidays; ticket 5 €*), founded by Cosimo il Vecchio, which has splendid illuminated manuscripts **(3)**. De-

(3)

signed by Michelangelo, the Laurentian Library was completed by Ammannati and Vasari. The public is admitted to the vestibule and the stunning triple stairway.

4. Cappelle Medicee

Piazza Madonna degli Aldobrandini 6, tel 055.2388602
For telephone bookings ring 055.294883
8.15am-5pm, closed 1st, 3rd and 5th Mon, 2nd and 4th Sun of the month.
Tickets 6 €, concessions 3 €

The entrance to the Medici Chapels, the dynasty's mausoleum, is

(4)

behind the basilica. The lavish marble decoration of the Princes' Chapel showcases the ability of the Opificio delle Pietre Dure. Michelangelo's New Sacristy (1521-24) recalls in its structure the Old Sacristy. Also by Michelangelo are the statues on the monuments to Giuliano Duke of Nemours, son of Lorenzo il Magnifico, and to Lorenzo Duke of

Urbino, grandson of the same **(4)**, as well as the *Madonna with Child* on the tomb of the "two Magnificents", Lorenzo and Giuliano.

5. Palazzo Medici-Riccardi

Via Cavour 3, tel 055.2760340
9-7pm; closed Wed
Ticket 4 €, concessions 2.50 €

Built by Michelozzo for Cosimo il Vecchio in 1444-1462, it is the prototype of the Florentine Renaissance *palazzo*. The Riccardi family bought it in 1659; today it is the seat of various government offices. The palace **(5)** had originally a loggia on the corner, that was walled up in 1517. Two "kneeling" windows (resting on corbels), said to have been designed by Michelangelo, were inserted: they would be

Chiostro dello Scalzo

Via Cavour 69
Tel 055.2388604
Mon, Thu and Sat 8.10am-1.50pm, entrance free
The cloister of the chapel belonging to a confraternity of flagellants commonly called "dello Scalzo" (i.e. barefoot), was decorated in 1509-26 by Andrea del Sarto with frescoes depicting scenes from the life of the Baptist. The cycle is considered one of his masterpieces and inspired all major Mannerist painters.

copied countless times in Florentine architecture. The court, once filled with statues, was decorated in the 18th century with "trophies" made of items from the Riccardi's archaeological collections. On the right is "Lorenzo's

(5)

(1)

and, on the third altar on the right, a 8th-century Byzantine Madonna. To the right of the church is the entrance to the monastery. Here lived Saint Antonino Pierozzi, Vicar General of the order and after 1446 bishop of Florence (his sarcophagus is in the sacristy), Girolamo Savonarola, who was

(2)

Chamber", where the Magnificent attended to business, now housing a state-of-the-art multimedia presentation. One stairway leads to the first-floor gallery, with a Luca Giordano fresco on the ceiling; the other to the palace's gem: the *Cappella dei Magi*, designed by Michelozzo and splendidly decorated by Benozzo Gozzoli (1459-60) with frescoes depicting the *Journey of the Magi* (1). The dazzling cortege, winding along three walls through a fairy-tale landscape, contains portraits of the Medici (including a ten-year old Lorenzo and his little brother Giuliano) and of their followers.

mo il Vecchio to the Dominicans in 1437. The 13th-century church and the monastery (2) were enlarged and much altered by Michelozzo; further alterations were made later, and the façade (3) dates from 1777-78. Of note inside the church are the Beato Angelico *Crucifix* above the main altar (1425-28)

6. Chiesa and Museo di San Marco

Piazza San Marco 1
Tel 055.2388608
For telephone bookings
ring 055.294883
Opening times of the museum:
Tue-Fri 8.30am-1.50pm, Sat
and Sun 8.30am-7pm; closed
2nd and 4th Mon, 1st and 3rd
Sun of the month; ticket 4 €

St Mark's, which belonged to the Sylvestrine order, was given by Cosi-

(3)

(5)

and the cells where Savonarola (4) lived, displaying images of his martyrdom and a well-known portrait by Fra' Bartolomeo. In the library, built by Michelozzo in 1441, rare illuminated manuscripts are on display. The former guest quarters on the ground floor house the few stones that were salvaged from the demolition of the old town centre.

7. Orto Botanico "Giardino dei Semplici"

Via P. A. Micheli 3
Tel 055.2757402
9-1pm, closed Wed; ticket 4 €
6-14s 1.50 €, under 6s free

The botanical garden (5), one of the oldest of its kind, was established in

prior of the monastery, Fra' (Friar) Bartolomeo, and most eminently Fra' Angelico (Fra' Giovanni da Fiesole), who worked here from 1443 to 1447. Owing to his frescoes and to the many paintings by him and by other artists of the age, this is one of the main museums in Florence. On the first floor are the cells frescoed by Fra' Angelico,

(4)

The university museums

Via G. La Pira 4
Info and bookings: tel 055.2756209 (Mon-Fri 9am-1pm)
info@museiscientificifiorentini.it
Joint ticket to all science museums available

Museo di Geologia e Paleontologia

9am-1pm; Sat until 5pm; closed Wed and national holidays. Ticket 4 €. Tel 055.2757536
The Geology and Palaeontology Museum has one of the main collections of fossils in Italy. The rooms that are open to the public display skeletons of mammals that once – surprisingly – roamed the area, such as two elephants, approx. 4 m (more or less 13 ft) tall, found in the Arno Valley (and familiarly called Linda and Pietro).

Museo di Mineralogia e Litologia

9am-1pm; Sat until 5pm; closed Wed and national holidays. Entrance free. Tel 055.2757537
The Mineralogy and Petrology

Museum boasts approx. 45,000 mineral specimens, also cut gems, often of remarkable size. But even visitors normally bored by mineralogy will be thrilled by the Medici collections: cups, vases, seals and caskets of exquisite workmanship, made of gems and semi-precious stones.

Museo Botanico

9am-1pm; Sat until 5pm (only by appointment); closed Wed and national holidays. Entrance free. Tel 055.2757462
With its 8 million specimens, the Botanical Museum is one of the most complete of its kind. Only the hall with the specimens, the wax models, the ancient herbals and botanical manuscripts is open to the public.

1545 by Cosimo I. Here one can admire sequoias, cedars and oak trees from the early 19th century, medicinal plants ("semplici") and tropical plants in hot and in temperate greenhouses. In spring, azaleas and other flowering plants fill it with a riot of colour.

8. Galleria dell'Accademia

Via Ricasoli 66 - Tel 055.2388609
8.15am-6.50pm; closed Mon.
For telephone bookings
ring 055.294883
Ticket 6.50 €, 18-26s half
price, under 18s and over 65s
free; joint ticket with Museo
dell'Opificio delle Pietre Dure
7 €, except when there are
temporary exhibitions

The gallery attached to the Academy of Fine Arts, founded in 1784 by Peter Leopold, owes its fame to the David **(1)** (1501-1504) and to other statues by Michelangelo: *St Matthew*, the four *Captives*, the *Palestrina Pietà*. And yet it also boasts an outstanding collection of paintings: Gothic and late Gothic panel paintings, works by Giotto's followers, by Lorenzo Monaco, Botticelli, Filippino Lippi and other 15th and 16th-century artists. The collection of

ancient Russian icons was donated by the Lorraine. Also of note is a painted wood panel, maybe belonging to a wedding chest, called Cassone degli Adimari, by an unknown 15th-century Florentine artist. On both sides of the Tribuna housing the David, paintings document the influence Michelangelo had on the artists of his age. Some rooms to the right of the entrance display a small but fine selection of ancient musical instruments, belonging to the conservatory "Luigi Cherubini" next door.

9. Museo dell'Opificio delle Pietre Dure

Via degli Alfani 78
Tel 055.265111
8.15am-2pm (Thu 8.15am-7pm);
closed Sun and holidays
Ticket 2 €, joint ticket with
Galleria dell'Accademia 7 €

Established by Ferdinando I mainly to provide the decoration for the Princes' Chapel, the Opificio (factory) is renowned world-wide for its exquisite workmanship in creating and restoring marble intarsia and sculptures in semi-precious stones **(2)**. The museum displays fine examples of its work in Medici and Lorraine times, also materials and instruments used.

(2)

10. Chiesa della SS. Annunziata

Piazza SS. Annunziata
Tel 055.266181
9am-noon and 4-5pm,
closed Wed; entrance free

The Church of the Most Holy Annunciation **(3)**, founded in 1250 and enlarged several times, contains a rich store of art. Its present structure dates from 1444-1477, the portico was added in 1601. Entrance is through the Chiostrino dei voti, which has fine frescoes by Pontormo, Andrea del Sarto and others.
The Baroque interior has a Volterrano painting (*c* 1670) on the ceiling; to the left, a sort of small temple houses an image believed to be miraculous, the *Annunciation* by an unknown 14th-century artist: according to the legend, the face of the Virgin was painted by an angel. The circular tribune, designed by Michelozzo, was completed by Leon Battista Alberti and later decorated by Giovan Battista Foggini. Also of note are

(1)

the frescoes in the chapels of the left aisle (Andrea del Castagno and Perugino) and in the Chiostro dei Morti (Andrea del Sarto). The square in front of the church, surrounded by porticoes, has an equestrian statue of Ferdinando I, by Giambologna (1608), and two fountains by Pietro Tacca (1629). It is one of the most harmonious and beautiful squares in Florence.

What about the children?

The kids are sick of churches and museums? The **Bottega dei Ragazzi** has toys, books, games that may be used freely (*Piazza SS. Annunziata, tel 055.2478386, Mon-Sat 9am-1pm/3-7pm, entrance free. A family member must stay with the child*).

11. Spedale degli Innocenti

Piazza SS. Annunziata
Tel 055.2491708
weekdays 8.30am-7pm, holidays 8.30am-2pm (last ticket sold 30 min before closing). Ticket 4 €, concessions 2 €.

The Foundling Hospital is noteworthy not just for its architecture and art, but because it is one of the oldest of its kind. The building was commissioned by the Silkmakers' Guild to Filippo Brunelleschi, and begun in 1419. The renowned glazed *tondi* depicting babies in swaddling clothes **(4)** are by Andrea della Robbia (1487). The "wheel" (a revolving cot) where babies could be left, was in use until 1875, and can be seen at the left end of the portico. On the first floor is the Pinacoteca: despite the sale of most bequests and donations in the 19th century, there are still **(5)** some remarkable paintings, such as a *Madonna with Child* by the young Botticelli and an *Adoration of the Magi* by Ghirlandaio. Opposite the portico is the Loggiato dei Serviti, by Antonio da Sangallo and Baccio d'Agnolo (1516).

12. Museo Archeologico **(4)**

Piazza SS. Annunziata 9
Tel 055.23575 - Mon 2-7pm; Tue and Thu 8.30am-7.30pm; Wed, Fri, Sat and Sun 8.30am-2pm. Ticket 4 €, concessions 2 € (last ticket sold 45 min before closing)

The Archaeological Museum in the 17th-century Palazzo della Crocetta originated from the Medici and the Lorraine collections, kept in the Uffizi until 1870. Its collection of Egyptian antiquities is second, in Italy, only to the Egyptian Museum's in Turin. Also remarkable is the Etruscan department, displaying urns, sculpture and bronzes. Of note are the Mater Matuta (5th century BC), the sarcophagus of Larthia Seianti (2nd century BC), the alabaster sarcophagus "of the Obese Man" (2nd century BC). Among the bronzes **(5)** are the *Arezzo Chimera* (4th century BC) and the *Small Idol*, which belonged to Cosimo I. The famous François Vase, an Attic krater dated 570 BC, was found in an Etruscan necropolis. Some Etruscan tombs discovered in the early 20th century have been reconstructed in the garden.

(3)

Albion Calzature
Via Nazionale 121a/r
Tel 055.282451

Albion has been designing footwear since 1952. Their shoes are sometimes "normal", more often flamboyant, but always entirely handmade, and can be customised on request. They even execute designs provided by clients!

Bojola
Via dei Rondinelli 25/r
Tel 055.211155

A historic shop selling leather bags, suitcases and accessories, close to the Via Tornabuoni.

Città San Gallo
Via Por Santa Maria 60/r
Tel 055.2396249

Established in 1922, this shop sells doilies, handkerchiefs, blouses, children's clothing and other items, all embroidered by hand or trimmed with traditional Tuscan handmade lace.

Echo
Via dell'Oriolo 37/r
Tel 055.2381149, open Sun

Two shops in one: head for the first "Echo" for that glamorous evening dress, or next door for jeans and trendy everyday wear. Prices are generally reasonable in both.

Giuditta Blandini Stile Biologico
Via dello Sprone 25/r
Tel 055.2776275
Viale M. Fanti 51/a
Tel 055.573400
Open throughout the day

Giuditta Blandini is an agronomist specialising in organic agriculture, and since 1977 has been making clothes for women, men and children, using only natural and organically grown material, such as hemp, silk, wool and linen, and natural dyes.

La luna e le stelle
Borgo S. Jacopo 17/r
Tel 055.214623

A shop that panders to mature women and to those who no longer wear size zero (or never did), by selling carefully tailored, stylish clothes for special occasions.

Luisa
Via Roma 19/r - Tel 055.217826

Its ever changing, always eccentric, and sometimes

Opening hours
Despite deregulation, most shops still observe the traditional opening hours, 9am-1pm/3.30-7.30pm, and are closed on Sunday and at least partly on Monday (some open in the afternoon, some not at all). In summer, afternoon opening hours are 4 to 8pm, and shops close on Saturday afternoon instead of Monday.

Shopping

Via Tornabuoni

Flanked by historic *palazzi*, this is the most exclusive shopping street in town. Sadly, in recent years it has lost many of the 19th-century establishments that made up its traditional charm (the restaurant Doney, the café Giacosa, the international bookshop Seeber, the English pharmacy). Together with nearby Via della Vigna Nuova it has increasingly become the street of the great fashion labels: Ferragamo, in the Palazzo Sini-Feroni at the end of the street closest to the Arno, Dior, Prada, Cavalli, Hermes, Gucci, and many more. At no. 64 Procacci is still holding out, with its vintage furniture and its renowned truffle sandwiches.

outrageous shop windows are legendary. Luisa sells womens- and menswear by world-famous labels.

Old England Stores
Via dei Vecchietti 25/R
Tel 055.211983

Established in 1924 to cater to the needs of the British expat community, this shop with the telling name was built by walling up an alley connecting Via dei Vecchietti to Via Brunelleschi. Everything on offer - clothing, perfumery, food - is absolutely British (they even sell "Duchy Originals", biscuits and preserves from Prince Charles's Duchy of Cornwall). The shop retains the original furnishings.

Pesci che volano
Borgo Pinti 27/r

A cosy little workshop where two young women knit incessantly to create colourful woollens: hats, sweaters, ponchos, bags, and more. And if you want a custom-made item, they will be happy to oblige.

A. Ugolini
Via Calzaiuoli 65/r
Tel 055.214439

It is an established fact that Florentines have always been Anglomaniacs. And Ugolini has been, for over a hundred years, a beacon of Anglophile attire: Ballantyne, Burberry, Church… combined with the very best of Italian fashion.

Furniture and Home Accessories

Martini
Via S. Verdiana 6/r
Tel 055.2480612

From basket to bookcase, from placemat to

rocking chair, all the bamboo and rattan items you can think of, also country-style furniture and accessories in wood.

Progetto Verde
Piazza T. Tasso 11/a
Tel 055.2998029

Building materials and furnishings for the environmentally conscious. They offer professional advice for an environmentally friendly home.

Samples
Via de' Bardi 23/r
Tel 055.2478872

A new, trendy place where to buy unique, limited edition furniture by European designers. They also sell bags, hats, home accessories.

Gifts

Bartolini
Via dei Servi 24-28/r
Tel 055.211895

Established in 1921, Bartolini has the widest range of kitchen- and tableware in town: from corkscrew to high quality crystal, to pots and pans for every need. If they don't have it, it doesn't exist.

Shopping

Ponte Vecchio

It is hard to visualise that long ago these shops were used by butchers and greengrocers, who threw their refuse into the river. Then Ferdinando I decreed that goldsmiths should take over the premises. Maybe he had a sensitive nose, and was bothered by the stench that penetrated even the Vasari Corridor? Tourists and locals, as they gaze at the sparkling shop windows, have reason to thank him.

Natura è
Via dello Studio 30/r
Tel 055.2657624

This is the place where to buy unusual gifts for nature lovers and science fans: windup radios, compasses, gardeners' kits, hygrometers, and clever games.

Pineider
Piazza Signoria 13-14/r
Tel 055.284655

Established in 1774, Pineider began by selling sta-

FONDATA NEL 1774

tionery and writing accessories. Their personalised letterheads, printed invitations, and business cards are legendary. They also sell desk accessories and briefcases.

International Crafts

Borgo Alegre
Via dei Serragli 88/r
Tel 055.2658299

Named Alegre in honour of Porto Alegre and the World Social Forum, this fair trade outlet is also "allegro" in the sense of cheerful, overflowing with clothes, toys, foods and crafts from all over the world, produced strictly according to the principles of fair trade. They also sell Italian organic food.

Marchi
Borgo degli Albizi 69/71r
Tel 055.2340415

From incense sticks to furniture, from ceramics to jewellery: all imports from the "fabulous Orient". The range of textiles, scarves, cushion covers, throws is particularly alluring.

Messico e Nuvole
Borgo degli Albizi 54/r
Tel 055.242677

On the threshold, a life-size (American) Indian invites passers-by to step inside.
The vast shop, which also boasts a fine courtyard, sells American Indian crafts: silver and turquoise jewellery, figurines, ceramics, shirts, and even furniture from Mexico.

A Yearly Appointment

La Mostra Mercato Internazionale dell'Artigianato
Fortezza da Basso,
Viale Strozzi 1;
info: Firenzefiera
tel 055.49721-4625205

Established in 1931, the International Crafts Fair quickly became an obligatory appointment for Florentines and visitors. Hundreds of Italian and foreign exhibitors gather in the grand Renaisssance Fortezza da Basso, to display textiles, accessories, jewellery, furnishings, gift items, food and wine, and a lot more besides. The fair stays open late into the night, and there are bars and restaurants inside. It is held approximately between 25 April and 1 May and is always unbelievably crowded (especially near the stands of "exotic" countries).

Shopping

Scandinavia
Via de' Ginori 23/r
Tel 055.289507

A fine shop specialising, as one can infer from its name, in Scandinavian gift items: candles in all hues, toys, sweaters, ceramics, Christmas decorations... also, everything you might need for cross-stitch embroidery.

Typical Florentine Crafts

Brandimarte
Viale L. Ariosto 11/r
Tel 055.23041

A renowned workshop specialising in silverware, from traditionally chiselled to smart modern items.

Cellini
Via S. Egidio 31/r
Tel 055.245335

Desk sets, boxes in all shapes and sizes, coin purses, frames and more: sturdy leather items made by hand to the high standard of traditional Florentine craftsmanship.

Ceramiche Luca della Robbia
Via del Proconsolo 19/r
Tel 055.283532, 10am-6.30pm

A shop with a challenging name. Established in 1904, in premises that are part of the Badia Fiorentina, it sells hand-decorated ceramics and reproductions of works of art. The originals are across the street, in the Bargello.

Le pietre nell'arte
Piazza Duomo 36/r
Tel 055.212587

Pictures, tables, jewellery in "commesso fiorentino", the traditional Florentine marble inlay, also jewellery made from semi-precious stones.

Sbigoli
Via Sant'Egidio 4/r
Tel 055.2479713

Established as long ago as 1850 (at the time they made building material and terracotta stoves), Sbigoli sells a wide range of terracotta pots and vases, and ceramics with traditional Florentine decoration, made in the workshop behind the shop.

Scuola del Cuoio
Piazza S. Croce
(through the church)
Via S. Giuseppe 5/r
(through the garden)
Tel 055.244533, winter: closed Sun, summer: open all week

The Leather School is in a league by itself: not just because of the fascinating premises (the dormitory designed by Michelozzo, in the monastery of S. Croce), but also because, as the name indicates, it is far more than a shop. Established in 1950, when Florence was struggling in the aftermath of war, it has trained generations of artisans. Nowadays the school offers also short-term courses – some lasting as little as half a day – to anyone who wishes to learn the basics of the ancient art of working leather. Visitors who only wish to shop will find a wide range of leather items (albums, frames, jewellery cases, handbags), all designed and made on the premises according to the best traditions of the craft.

Ugolini
Lungarno Acciaioli 60-70/r
Tel 055.284969,
winter: closed Sun and Mon,
summer: open all week

Established in 1868, this workshop has been

keeping alive the ancient tradition of "pietra dura", also called Florentine mosaic, making panels, table tops and other items with exquisite inlays.

Scuola del Cuoio®
LEATHER SCHOOL®

Shopping

Paper and Supplies

Marzotto
Borgo degli Albizi 86/r
Tel 055.2340726

This colourful shop/storeroom, housed since 1890 in the splendid Palazzo Ramirez di Montaldo (1558), sells a wide range of paper and cardboard items. Despite severe damage suffered during the flood of 1966, it has salvaged some of the original furniture.

Rigacci
Via dei Servi 71/r
Tel 055.216206

This superbly well-stocked art supplies shop boasts among its past and present clients several renowned artists, as indicated by the paintings on display. Unfortunately, all the original furnishings were lost in the flood of 1966.

Zecchi
Via dello Studio 19/r
Tel 055.211470, closed Sat afternoon

A historic shop selling art supplies and materials for the restoration of works of art. A veritable treasure-trove for the art lover. In this very building the first university of Florence, the "Studio Fiorentino", was established in 1348.

Herbalists and Pharmacies

Erboristeria Spezieria "Palazzo Vecchio" Dr. Di Massimo
Via Vaccherecia 9/r
Tel 055.2396055, 9am-7pm, Sun 3.30-7.30pm

Next to Palazzo Vecchimo, and flanked by flashier neighbours, this tiny shop is easy to overlook, but it would be a pity. We recommend a leisurely stop to sniff and choose among its extraordinary range of perfumes and eaux de perfum, in classic or exotic fragrances. They also sell own-made beauty and body care products.

De Herbore
Via del Proconsolo 43/r
Tel 055.211706

A vast, extremely well-stocked herbalist selling all sorts of things, from herbal teas to skin care products, to organic food.

Farmacia del Cinghiale
Piazza del Mercato Nuovo 4/r
Tel 055.282128

Established in the 18th century, by the 19th century this pharmacy had become a meeting place for intellectuals. They

still make body care products using traditional recipes and natural ingredients.

Farmacia SS. Annunziata
Via dei Servi 80/r
Tel 055.210738

First mentioned in 1561, the pharmacy was soon granted the honour of styling itself Grand Ducal Apothecary. They still prepare galenicals and body care products, combining tradition and modern scientific knowledge. Note the fine cabinets.

Officina Profumo Farmaceutica S. Maria Novella
Via della Scala 16
Tel 055.216276

Adjoining Piazza Santa Maria Novella is one of the world's most ancient pharmacies, established by Dominican monks as far back as the 13th century. Here, in rooms splendidly decorated with frescoes and ancient cabinets, one can buy perfumes, creams, liqueurs and other products, still prepared according to the monks' old recipes.

Shopping

Plants and Flowers

Fiori della Signoria
Piazza della Signoria 37/r
Tel 055.2698658,
closed Sun afternoon

A riot of colour beside Palazzo Vecchio. The owners of this splendid florist shop are reliable and friendly, and have a second shop in the grand Palazzo Gondi (*Piazza San Firenze 1*).

Giardino di Annalena
Via Romana 36
Tel 055.2335028, closed Sun

Exactly opposite one of the entrances to Boboli, a gate bearing the inscription *Horti Annalenae* leads to a secret garden, fragrant and many-hued: this nursery has a truly unforgettable charm.

Giardino Torrigiani
Via dei Serragli 146
Tel 055.224527

In the 16th century this large private garden was used as a kitchen garden. It was redesigned in its present form in the early 19th century. Part of it is now a nursery and sells garden and house plants, and tropical plants.

Food and Drink

Casa del Vino
Via dell'Ariento 16/r
Tel 055.483215

Once a modest wine shop, it is now a well-stocked wine merchant with over 900 wines from all over the world on offer. The solid walnut furniture dates from the mid-19th century.

Fratelli Zanobini
Via Sant'Antonino 47/r
Tel 055.2396850, 8am-2pm, 3.30-8pm

A historic shop in the San Lorenzo area. They sell wine produced by the owners and bottled in the traditional container for Chianti, the *fiasco*, spirits, and other liquors. They also serve wine by the glass and have maintained the old shop window.

Kosher market
Via dei Pilastri 7a/r
Tel 055.240508
Sun-Thu 8.30am-1.30pm/3-8pm, Fri 8.30am-one hour before Shabbat, closed Sat

Jewish food of the Sephardi (Mediterranean and Middle Eastern) tradition, produced under strict rabbinical supervision.

Pegna
Via dello Studio 8
Tel 055.282701,
closed Wed afternoon
(Sat afternoon in summer)

Florentines and foreign visitors have flocked to

Pegna for their food since 1860, knowing they would not be disappointed. A stone's throw from the cathedral, the shop boasts 7000 products that can satisfy every need: typical Tuscan salami, cheeses, sauces from all over the world, oil, wine, preserves and a lot more.

Oleum Olivae
Via S. Egidio 22r
Tel 055.2001092

Alberto and Margherita are a young couple who has decided to bet on oil and high-quality typical products, opening a spe-

cialised shop where one can find the very best extra-virgin olive oil from all Italian regions, choice balsamic vinegar,

Shopping

Markets

Mercato Centrale di San Lorenzo

The covered food market (*Mon-Sat 7am-2pm; in winter also Sat afternoon*) is housed in a fine, greenhouse-like structure (1870-74), and is surrounded by an open-air market selling clothes, leather goods and souvenirs. Inside one can eat well and at reasonable prices at "da Nerbone".

Mercato di Sant'Ambrogio
7am-2pm, closed Sun
Food and clothes market (where with luck one can find some convenient buy). Inside, at "da Rocco", the food is good and cheap.

Mercato delle Pulci
Piazza dei Ciompi
9am-1pm/3-6pm, closed Sun, in winter Mon as well
Here one can find anything, furniture, knick-knacks, books, postcards, dolls, vintage clothing. On the last Sunday of the month the stands stay open, and the flea market overflows into the adjoining streets.

Mercato del Porcellino
Loggiato del Porcellino,
Via Porta Rossa
Tue-Sun 9am-7.30pm
(9am-8pm in summer)
This is a market almost exclusively for tourists, nor could it be otherwise, seeing where it is located!

Mercato delle Cascine
Viale Lincoln, Tue 8am-2pm
Clothes, shoes, food... It's a long, long walk from one end to the other, and in summer one had better go early to avoid the heat. Locals love it, because rummaging through the second-hand clothes, or hunting for cutting edge fashions, there is always the chance to stumble upon some really good buy.

Markets in Piazza Santo Spirito
"Arti e mestieri d'Oltrarno": 2nd Sun of the month; Crafts and Second-Hand Market
"Fierucola": 3rd Sun of the month, except Aug and Dec.
A lively "alternative" market: organic vegetables, cheese, honey and much more, sold directly by producers; also crafts and fair trade stalls.

and genuine Tuscan products such as pulses, cheese, organic preserves. It is also the ideal place to come to for a fantastic sandwich.

Bartolucci
Via Condotta 12/r
Tel 055.211773
Borgo dei Greci 11A/r
Tel 055.2398596

Cheerful toys, funny clothes hangers, clocks, knick-knacks, all strictly handmade from wood.

Dreoni
Via Cavour 31/r (rear entrance via Ginori 36-38/r), tel 055.216611

A historic shop, in front of whose large windows generations of Florentines (children and grown-ups alike) have stood gaping. Their range of toys and cuddly animals surpasses imagination, and

don't miss the model department!

La città del sole
Via de' Cimatori 21r
Tel 055.2776372

A great shop for traditional toys, such as kites, puppets, kaleidoscopes, and models to build.

Libreria Antiquaria Gonnelli
Via Ricasoli 14/r
Tel 055.216835
Founded by Luigi

Shopping

Gonnelli in 1875, this is one of the oldest antiquarian bookshops still in operation in Italy. Scholars and connoisseurs can find manuscripts, ancient books, drawings and prints.

Libreria Art & Libri
Via dei Fossi 32/r
Tel 055.264186

This shop specialises in art books: their selection is excellent, and they will be happy to track down any out-of-print book for you.

Libreria Antiquaria Ippogrifo
Via della Vigna Nuova 5/r
Tel 055.290805

A tiny antiquarian bookshop focusing mainly on the history of Florence and Tuscany.

Antique dealers in Via Maggio and Via dei Fossi

In a town whose claim to fame is based on the arts and the crafts of past ages, there is obviously no lack of antique dealers – from hopeful second-hand shops to the most exclusive galleries. But a walk along Via dei Fossi and Via Maggio is a feast for the eyes. The shop windows, belonging to solidly established antique dealers, forms a sort of open-air museum. Often, moreover, and especially in Via Maggio, these shops occupy splendid premises in historic palaces. In Via Maggio the focus is on furniture, sculpture, Italian and Tuscan paintings from the 15th to the early 19th century, with few exceptions (such as Daniele Boralevi at no. 84/r, Oriental carpets, or Piselli Balzano at no. 23/r, ancient textiles). Via dei Fossi is the place to go to for more recent items, such as 17th to 20th century paintings, and particularly Macchiaioli (La Stanzina, at no. 51/r.).

Salimbeni
Via M. Palmieri 14-16/r
Tel 055.2340905

Established in 1948, it has become a haven for scholars and connoisseurs. In an age when bookstores increasingly tend to resemble supermarkets, it's nice to have someone advise you competently. The shop specialises in art and antiquarian books and has a good selection of books on Tuscan history and traditions.

Music

Discoteca fiorentina
Via dell'Oriolo 1-3/r
Tel 055.2340854

A very ample choice of CDs and DVDs: mainly classical music, but also the latest pop releases. The owners, two friendly red-haired sisters, are on hand to advise customers expertly.

Ricordi Media Store
Via Brunelleschi 8/r
Tel 055.214104

Three floors of CDs, videogames, videos, DVDs. Always crowded with youngsters in search of the latest releases.

Rock Bottom
Via degli Alfani 34-36/r
Tel 055.245220

The right place for those who continue to prefer vinyl to CDs, and for fans of 1960s to 1980s music. The owners are very knowledgeable.

Twisted Jazz Shop
Borgo San Frediano 21/r
Tel 055.282011

The only shop in town dedicated entirely to jazz. Records, videos, posters and scores: it's a paradise for jazz enthusiasts and for those wishing to become one.

Bistecca alla fiorentina (T-bone steak), *ribollita* (vegetable and bread soup), *pappa al pomodoro* (bread and tomato soup), *trippa* (tripe), *fagioli all'uccelletto* (white beans with tomato and sage) ... Florentine cuisine is considered "poor" (and so it was, originally), but is made with simple, genuine ingredients.

Many trattorias and restaurants are proud to serve it. Other establishments specialise in creative cuisine, while ethnic and fish restaurants are on the increase.

Prices obviously vary. When looking at the menu displayed outside a restaurant, watch out for "coperto" (cover) and "servizio" (service), as they are not always included, and may considerably affect the bill. Where "average price" has been indicated, this refers to a full meal (starters, first and main course, or first and main course and a dessert), drinks not included.

Restaurants, cafés & more

Haute Cuisine

Alle Murate
*Via del Proconsolo 16/r
Tel 055.240618, open 8pm-midnight, closed Mon and for lunch*

This renowned restaurant has now moved to the historic *palazzo* of the Judges' and Notaries' Guild (before dinner one can admire the frescoes with the help of a multilingual audio guide). Elegant ambience, dimmed lights, and one of the best regional cuisines in Tuscany. Ample choice of wines. Average price 45-55 €.

Enoteca Pinchiorri
Via Ghibellina 87, tel 055.242757, closed Sun-Wed for lunch

Undoubtedly one of the most famous restaurants in town, well-known by all for its stunning cuisine, its stunning wine list (they boast the best-stocked cellar in Europe) and their equally stunning prices (over 200 €).

Il Cibreo
*Via de' Macci 118/r
Tel 055.2341100,
closed Sun and Mon;
booking advisable*

This is not just a restaurant, it's a local legend. The owner, Fabio Picchi, is a well-known personality in Florence and

abroad, and the restaurant is considered one of the best in town. Average price 65-70 €. The lower-priced **Cibreino**, the adjoining trattoria, has some of the same dishes on the menu. Across the street is **Caffè Cibreo**, a small café also serving light meals.

La Giostra
Borgo Pinti 12/r, tel 055.241341, closed for lunch Sat and Sun; booking advisable

Tucked away in the centre of town, this little restaurant is well known to lovers of high-quality cuisine. The owner and chef is a real prince, Dimitri Alberto Leopoldo of Hapsburg: expect therefore a Tuscan menu with Austrian touches. For a glorious finale, try the *Imperial Sacher Torte*. Average price 80 €.

Osteria del Caffè Italiano
*Via Isola delle Stinche 11-13/r
Tel 055.289368, closed Mon*

Half restaurant, half wine bar, serving delicate dishes inspired by the Tuscan tradition and wine by the glass. The

menu changes frequently and always includes at least one vegetarian option. The tiny pizzeria next door makes a delicious takeaway Neapolitan pizza (there are also a few tables, but the wait for a free one tends to be very long). Lunch about 40 €, pizza 7-8 €.

Italian Cuisine

Acqua al 2
*Via della Vigna Vecchia 40/r
(at the corner with Via dell'Acqua)
Tel 055.284170, open every day
7pm- 1am*

The perfect after-theatre place (and you stand a good chance of spotting the actors just seen on the stage). We recom-

A table with a view

La Loggia
*Piazzale Michelangelo 1
Tel 055.2342832*
The Neo-Classical building, designed by Poggi (who meant it for a museum), overlooks Piazzale Michelangelo and Florence. One can eat in the fine inner rooms, on the magnificent loggia, in the garden or on the terrace. Tuscan cuisine and an impressive wine list. Average price 100 €.

Villa Aurora
*Piazza Mino 39, Fiesole
Tel 055.59363.*
This 19th-century villa, where royalty were once entertained, is now the Hotel Villa Aurora. Its restaurant boasts a truly breath-taking panorama, especially from the terrace. Modern Tuscan cuisine, average price about 43 €.

mend: "assaggi di primi" (selection of pasta dishes), "tagliata all'arancio" (orange flavoured, thinly sliced steak), the salads. Average price 20-25 €. Next door, **La Via dell'Acqua** (*tel 055.290748*) serves simpler fare for a quick lunch, an *aperitivo*, or a light dinner.

Angels
Via del Proconsolo 29-31/r
Tel 055.2398762

This smart restaurant and wine bar, a stone's throw from the Duomo, serves traditional local dishes, intriguingly revisited. *Aperitivo*: sushi on Tuesdays, ethnic on Thursdays. Buffet lunch 12 €, starters and first courses 15-20 €, mains 20 €, desserts 8.50 €.

Baldovino
Via San Giuseppe 22/r
(Piazza S. Croce) - Tel 055.241773

It's more like a tavern, friendly but crowded. Tuscan dishes, but also salads, fish, pizza from the wood-fired oven; wine by the glass. Prices from 18-20 € up. The **wine bar** across the street (*Enoteca, at no.18/r, tel 055.2347220*) boasts a

list of over 1000 Italian wines.

Beccofino
Piazza degli Scarlatti 1/r
(lungarno Guicciardini)
Tel 055.290076; closed Mon and for lunch (except Sun)

Stylish restaurant and wine bar with river-view terrace. Tuscan and Mediterranean cuisine and a long wine list. Starters and first courses 9.50 €, mains with side dish 20.50 €, desserts 6.50 €.

Birreria Centrale 1898
Piazza de' Cimatori 1/r
Tel 055.211915, noon-2.30pm, 7-11pm, closed Sun

Restaurant, wine bar and pub all in one, in a 14th-century palace overlooking a picturesque square. The menu includes typical South-Tyrolean and Bavarian dishes. Try the unfiltered beers from independent breweries. Starters and first courses 5-9 €, typical dishes 12 €.

Boccanegra
Via Ghibellina 124/r
Tel 055.2001098,
closed for lunch and Sun

A fascinating restaurant opposite the Teatro Ver-

di: antique furniture and creative dishes prepared with typical regional ingredients. Starters and first courses 13-19 €, mains 18-24 €, desserts 5 €. Around the corner (*via Verdi 27/r*) is the **Enoteca del Boccanegra**, where one can indulge in wine tasting while eating a light meal. **The Cantinetta** del Boccanegra adjoining the restaurant offers pizza baked in the wood-fired oven and wine by the glass.

Buca dell'Orafo
Via dei Girolami 28/r
Tel 055.213619, closed Sun and Mon for lunch

Named after the jewellers' workshops that once dotted the area close to Ponte Vecchio, the restaurant is picturesquely located under an arch, in a narrow street leading to Piazza della Signoria. Starters 6-8 €, first courses 9 €, mains 13-17 €, cover 2.50 €.

Filipepe
Via San Niccolò 43
Tel 055.2001397,
closed for lunch

New Mediterranean cuisine: hot and cold plates, a fine selection of cheese, crisp salads, and desserts beloved by patrons. Average price 25 €.

Restaurants, cafés & more

Finisterrae
Via dei Pepi 3-5/r
Tel 055.263875,
closed for lunch

A friendly, atmospheric restaurant, specialising in the cuisine of countries bordering the Mediterranean. Average price 20-25 €. The bar serves *meze* and *tapas*. The menu is less varied at lunchtime, but one can eat outside, in Piazza Santa Croce.

Il Canapone Club
Via Mazzetta 5a
Tel 055.2381729; 7-11pm, Sun brunch noon-3pm, closed Mon

Close to Piazza Santo Spirito, a quaint, candle-lit restaurant, furnished with chairs of every description. The menu changes every week, and includes vegetarian dishes. First courses 6-9 €, mains 13-19 €, desserts 5-8 € (cover 2 €). Sunday buffet brunch 18 €. Annual membership card 2 €.

Le Barrique
Via del Leone 40/r
Tel 055.224192, 7pm-midnight, closed for lunch and Mon

Serves unusual dishes such as liver pâté with blackberry preserve or radicchio-filled ravioli in pumpkin cream soup. Good open wines. Average price 25-30 €.

OiO
Piazza Piattellina 7/r
Tel 055. 212917,
Tue-Sat 9am-9pm, closed Mon

A friendly bar with kitchen that serves nourishing snacks late at night (salads, *carpaccio*, cheese), made with organic products (6-8 €), also an excellent organic wine and cocktails (7 €).

Osteria Santo Spirito
Piazza Santo Spirito 16/r
Tel 055.2382383; open every day, and throughout the day from Apr to Oct, booking advisable

One can sit inside or in the garden overlooking the square, and eat Tuscan and other regional dishes, cheese plates, mouth-watering desserts. Starters about 8 €, first courses 6-9 € (with fish 9-16 €), mains 12-20 (fish 16-20 €), desserts 5 €.

Vinai (also called "Vinaini")

These "wine places" where one can drink a glass of wine and eat a snack are an endangered species. Many of those who have managed to survive have done so by adapting, and are now less genuine, and more up-market.

Antico Vinaio di Firenze

I Fratellini
dal 1875

Tel. 055/2396096
Via dei Cimatori, 38/r - FIRENZE

Antico Noè
Volta di San Pietro 6/r
Tel 055.2340838
Open for lunch and dinner closed Sun

The clientele is very mixed: penniless students, tourists looking for local colour, and aficionados, who prefer a glass of wine to a cappuccino even at breakfast time … Adjoining the "vinaino" is a pleasant room where one can eat traditional Tuscan dishes, and drink a good Chianti.

I fratellini
Via dei Cimatori 38/r
8am-8pm

Practically a hole in the wall. Customers eat and drink in the street, small shelves are provided for the glasses. Sandwiches about 2 €.

I' Vinaino
Via Palazzuolo 124/r
Tel 055.292287
closed Sun

A friendly place where to eat lunch or dinner, or just sip a glass of wine and eat a snack. Open from early morning (as a café) to late at night. First courses 6-7 €, mains 8 €, salads 6.50 €. Dishes for less than 6 € available for lunch.

La Mescita
Via degli Alfani 707r
8am-4.30pm

It started in 1927 as a shop selling wine and oil, and a "wine-pouring place". It is one of the most genuine *vinai* in town, serving simple food at convenient prices. Sandwiches 1.60-3 €, first courses 4 €.

Restaurants, cafés & more

Tuscan Cuisine Trattorias

Antica Mescita San Niccolò

Via San Niccolò 60/r
Tel 055.2342836, closed Sun.

In a charming corner of town, one of the few remaining *mescitas* (literally "wine-pouring place") with kitchen attached. Perfect for a light dinner or after-theatre meal. Tasting dishes 8-12 €, wine 2-5 € the glass. Buffet lunch less than 10 €.

Antico Fattore

Via Lambertesca 1-3/r
Tel 055.288975, closed Sun

This restaurant behind the Uffizi was in the 1930s a meeting place for artists and writers, and the venue of a literary award. Gutted by the car bomb in 1993, it has been brought back to life. The cuisine is excellent: try *rigaglie alla salvia* (chicken giblets with sage), or *involtini di carne e carciofo* (meat and artichoke roulades). Starters 5-8 €, first courses 6.20-7.20 €, mains 9.50-14 €, side dishes 4.50 €.

Buca San Giovanni

Piazza S. Giovanni 8
Tel 055.287616, closed Mon

Opened in 1882 in the former sacristy of the Battistero, the restaurant serves traditional Tuscan dishes in a highly evocative ambience. There is even a fresco by a follower of Giotto, and the bar counter used to be an altar. Live music after 9pm. Average price 36-40 €.

Coco Lezzone

Via del Parioncino 26/r
Tel 055.28712, closed Sun and Tue evening

An ancient tavern turned *trattoria*, that still has part of the original furnishings, and serves high-quality, traditional Tuscan cuisine. Average price 35-40 €.

Dino

Via Ghibellina 47/r
Tel 055.241452, closed Sun and Mon for lunch

An elegant restaurant not far from the Bargello. Tuscan cuisine, with ancient dishes such as spelt soup or sweet-and-sour wild boar. Own-made desserts and large wine-list. Starters 5-10 €, first courses 7-14, mains from 12 € up, cover 3 €.

Il Cantinone

Via Santo Spirito 6/r
Tel 055.218898, closed Mon

A steep flight of steps leads to an authentic cellar with vaulted ceiling. Traditional Tuscan cuisine, with bread baked in

a wood-fired oven and Chianti wines. Prices between 16 and 18 €.

Il Latini

Via dei Palchetti 6/r
Tel 055.210916, closed Mon

This crowded, family-run restaurant is a corner of old Tuscany, serving traditional dishes (*ribollita*, *bistecca*, *tiramisu*) at long wooden tables. Since 1982 they have been sponsoring the literary award "Amici del Latini". Starters 4-6 €, first courses 5-7 €, mains 13-20 €, desserts 6 €.

La Casalinga

Via dei Michelozzi 9/r
Tel 055.218624, closed Sun

An authentic family-run *trattoria*, established 1957, where dishes are still cooked as grandmother did. Desserts are traditional too: *cantuccini col vinsanto* (almond biscuits with dessert wine) and *schiacciata con l'uva* (a sort of grapes tart). Basic décor and rock-bottom prices.

Restaurants, cafés & more

La Pentola dell'Oro
Via di Mezzo 24/r
Tel 055.241808, closed Sun

In the evening this is the reign of Giuseppe Alessi, not just a cook, but a student of Medieval and Renaissance cooking: each dish has a rich history, each ingredient has been carefully researched (average price about 45 €). At lunchtime it becomes **Bettolino**, and serves more basic meals: mains 7 €, complete meal about 14 €.

Pallottino
Via Isola delle Stinche 1/r
Tel 055.289573, closed Mon
Booking advisable.

The best of Tuscan cuisine: *pappa al pomodoro, ribollita*, and the famous lard from Colonnata, cured in marble basins. Starters about 6 €, first courses about 7 €, mains about 9 €.

4 Leoni
Via dei Vellutini 1/r
Tel 055.218562 - meals served until 11pm, closed Wed for lunch

A typical Tuscan *trattoria*: straw covered chairs, stone walls, brick arches, and a matching menu, based mainly on steak and *tagliata*. Average price 25-30 €.

TRATTORIA 4 LEONI

Sabatino
Via Pisana 2/r
(Porta San Frediano)
Tel 055.225955,
closed Sat and Sun

Despite moving to new premises, Sabatino's ambience, menu, and prices have not changed. It still attracts the usual mix: a young "alternative" crowd, a few tourists, and the faithful. Shared tables and Tuscan cuisine at rock-bottom prices. Wine is "a consumo" (they put the bottle on the table and then gauge how much is missing).

Tre Merli
Via dei Fossi 12/r, tel 055.287062

A lively restaurant serving solid Tuscan fare (soups, stewed wild boar, steak), with wine and oil from San Gimignano, and homemade ice cream from Impruneta (two locations south of Florence). Lunch 10-12 €, dinner 25-35 €.

Fish

Fuor d'acqua
Via Pisana 37/r, tel 055.222299,
closed Sun and for lunch

A modish restaurant close to Porta San Frediano. The fish arrives fresh every day

"Trippa" and "lampredotto"

Trippai (tripe sellers) are worthy representatives of Florentine traditions: *trippa* and *lampredotto*, together with a good glass of wine, have been since time immemorial the lunch, dinner, morning or afternoon snack of craftsmen and labourers, who gather around the stall to eat and debate all kinds of topics: as a result the more genuine "trippai" have turned into political analysts, sports commentators, and experts on local events.
Trippa is made from the cow's forestomachs, and is usually served with a large amount of tomato sauce.
Lampredotto is from the stomach proper; it is boiled in broth together with herbs and tomato, then cut in fine strips, placed in a *panino* (bread roll), and seasoned with salt, pepper, chili pepper and *salsa verde*, a green sauce based on parsley, anchovies and capers.
Trippai are generally open every day except Sunday, more or less from 7-8am to 7-8pm. Prices for sandwiches, tripe and first courses are approximately 2.50 to 4 € (in any case never more than 5 €).

Il Trippaio del Porcellino
Piazza del Mercato Nuovo

Pollini
Via dei Macci (close to Piazza Sant'Ambrogio)
Il Trippaio di Borgo San Frediano
Borgo San Frediano (near Piazza de' Nerli)
I' Trippaio di Firenze
Via Maso da Finiguerra (at the corner of via Palazzuolo)
L'Antico Trippaio
Piazza de' Cimatori

Restaurants, cafés & more

from Viareggio and is famously prepared. Try the first courses, the shellfish, and the fish fry. Average price 60-70 €.

Lobs
Via Faenza 75-77/r
Tel 055.212478

A friendly, colourful tavern near San Lorenzo. Great mains, scrumptious desserts and an extensive list of white wines. First courses 15-18 €, mains 25 €.

Ricchi
Piazza Santo Spirito 8/r
Tel 055.280830
7.30-11pm, closed Sun (except 2nd Sun of the month). Book!

This renowned Oltrarno restaurant has a menu comprising only fresh fish. First courses 9-13 €, mains 15-20 €, desserts 5-6 €. Quick, non-fish menu for lunch.

Ethnic cuisine

Dioniso
Via San Gallo 16/r, tel 055.217882
A cheerful (and crowded) restaurant serving a genuinely Greek cuisine (the owner was born in

Florence from Greek parents). It is not uncommon for waiters and clients to suddenly stage a *sirtaki* exhibition. Average price 25 €. They have recently opened a takeaway (*Via dell'Agnolo 93 r*).

Eito
Via dei Neri 72/r
Tel 055.210940, closed Mon and for lunch (except Sat)

This is the oldest Japanese restaurant in Florence. Established in 1986, it has been recently refurbished in fiery red. The helpful Japanese staff will be happy to assist in choosing from the rich menu. Average price 40 €.

Haveli
Viale Fratelli Rosselli 31-33/r
Tel 055.355695

Friendly restaurant serving tasty North Indian cuisine. Average price 26-30 €.

Marina
Via Verdi 12/r, tel 055.2001736
open noon-3am

Near Piazza S. Croce, a very friendly, family-run restaurant serving Russian specialities, plus

a variety of Italian and Eastern European dishes. Starters 3.30-7 €, first courses about 5 €, mains 5-7 €. Convenient set lunches.

Il Mandarino
Via Condotta 17/r
Tel 055.2396130, closed Mon

One of the best Chinese restaurants in town. Good cuisine and attentive service. Starters and vegetables 2-4 €, first courses 3-6 €, mains 5-10 €, cover 1.50 €; set meal 12 €.

India
Viale Gramsci 43a, Fiesole
Tel 055.599900, booking required; 7.30-11.30pm, closed Tue

Rich Mughal cuisine, North Indian specialities such as *tandoori* dishes, also many vegetables and different kinds of bread. Average price about 25 €.

Momoyama
Borgo San Frediano 10/r
Tel 055.291840
8-11.30pm, Sun brunch 1-4pm

Japanese cuisine and "inventive food", an ever changing menu, and art exhibitions, are the features of this *sushi-bar*.

Restaurants, cafés & more

Excellent desserts and ice cream. Dishes from 12 €, Japanese dishes from 7 €, medium sushi 21 €.

Peking
Via del Melarancio 21/r
Tel 055.282922

The place tends to be packed with Chinese regulars: therefore we make so bold as to claim that the cooking is as authentic as it is tasty. There is the customary ample choice of dishes, at very moderate prices. Set meal for two 19 €.

Rose's Café
Via del Parione 26/r
Tel 055.287090
closed Sun for lunch

Breakfast, lunch, *aperitivo*, dinner... Rose's has the right dish for every occasion. A treat are the sushi and other Japanese dishes (dinner only, Monday excluded). Cocktails served late into the night. Quick lunch 11-13 €, dinner 35-40 €.

Sésame
Via delle Conce 20/r
Tel 055.2001381
closed for lunch

A restaurant with a great ambience, serving a perfect combination of traditional French cuisine and typical North African dishes. Lots of spicy fish and meat dishes. In summer one can dine in the garden. First

courses 5-9 €, mains 8-16 €, desserts 5 €.

Wine bars

Frescobaldi
Via de' Magazzini 2-4/r
Tel 055.284724; noon-2.30pm/ 7pm-midnight, closed for lunch Sun and Mon

The windows of this restaurant and wine bar, owned by the well-known Tuscan winemakers, open onto an alley close to Palazzo Vecchio. Italian and Tuscan dishes, matched with selected wines. First courses 8-11 €, mains 12-16 €. Around the corner in Via Condotta is **Frescobaldino**, serving wine by the glass and Italian-style *tapas* (*noon-midnight*).

Fuori Porta
Via Monte alle Croci 10/r
Tel 055.2342483

A typical tavern, with alfresco tables and an enchanting view over the ancient city wall. One can eat or simply drink a glass of wine among friends.

Le volpi e l'uva
Piazza dei Rossi 1/r
Tel 055.2398132
11am-9pm, closed Sun

Half-way between the

Ponte Vecchio and the Pitti Palace, this is the place where to stop for Italian or French wine, in front of a plate of cheese or sliced salami. Wine by the glass 2-6 €.

Pizzerias

Il Pizzaiuolo
Via de'Macci 113/r
Tel 055.241171, closed Sun. Book!

Close to the Sant'Ambrogio market, this place serves the true pizza, with a thick crust and mozzarella made from water buffalo milk, baked in a wood-fired brick oven. The entire menu is typically Neapolitan: pasta with vegetables, fish, desserts and the obligatory lemon liqueur. First courses and pizza 5.50-9 €, fish courses 7.50-12.

Rossopomodoro
Piazza del Mercato Centrale 22
Tel 055.211131

Everything here is Neapolitan, from the ingredients to the "native language" menu. Many unusual pizzas (*Cafuncella, Sorrentina, Vesuvio …*). Also first courses and, depending on what is available on the market, a fish course. Pizza from 6-10 €.

Santa Lucia
Via Ponte alle Mosse 102/r
Tel 055.353255, closed Wed

One of the best pizzerias in town, renowned for its thick-crust pizza (ask

Restaurants, cafés & more

for "pasta alta" when you order). People queue in the street: you had better book.

Vico del Carmine
Via Pisana 40-42/r
Tel 055.2336862

Everything in this pizzeria close to Porta San Frediano has been arranged so as to re-create the ambience of a Neapolitan alley. Ingredients all come from Campania (mozzarella *di bufala*, sausages, even the wine) and the pizza crust is thick and soft as required by true Neapolitan tradition. Pizza 4.50-8 €, first courses from 7 €, mains from 12 €.

Yellow Bar
Via del Proconsolo 39/r
Tel 055.211766, closed Tue

Pub-style pizzeria with long tables, crowded at lunchtime, dinnertime, and after dinner. Starters about 6 €, first course 7-8 €, mains 10 €, pizza 7 €.

Vegetarian

Il Vegetariano
Via delle Ruote 30/r
Tel 055.475030

First courses, salads, mains, great desserts – plentiful helpings, moderate prices: you'll love this friendly place.

Customers lay their own tables and in summer can eat in the small walled garden.

Ruth's
Via Farini 2/a, tel 055.2480888
12.30-2.30pm/8-10.30pm,
closed Fri night and Sat

Next to the synagogue, a tiny kosher restaurant serving Mediterranean and Middle-Eastern dishes. Starters 6.50 €, first courses 7 €, mains 12 €.

Bakeries

Forno Galli
Via Bufalini 31-33/r - (7am-3am)
Via Faenza 39/r - (7am-8pm)

Focaccia, pizza, deli-

Ethnic fast food

Some tips on how to quell your hunger as you walk around town, and at the same time discover exotic flavours without great loss of time or money. Recently a great many shops selling Arab-style sandwiches, *kebab* etc, have sprung up. Many are disappointing, of indifferent quality and with little choice of dishes. Here are some "historic" places, and the best among the new entries. By law, they all ought to close by midnight, but....

Amon
Via Palazzuolo 26-28/r, tel 055.293146,
noon-3pm/6-11pm,
closed Sun

This has been the very first place to introduce Florentines to traditional Arab and Egyptian snacks, such as pita bread, falafel or *shawarma* (meat roasted on a vertical spit). No tables, alas!

El Taco
Via dei Benci 47/r
Tel 055.241970
12.30pm/midnight,
Fri and Sat open
until 3am

Small, colourful takeaway serving (you guessed it) true Mexican tacos. You can determine the level of hotness by choosing the sauce. Tacos 3.50-5 €, Mexican beer 3.50 €.

La Siesta
Via Magazzini 5/r,
10.30am-10.30pm

Close to Piazza Signoria, this place serves sandwiches with meat, *falafel* or vegetable fillings (3-4 €), also dishes complete with rice, meat and vegetables (5-7 €). The place is well kept, the food is good, and there are even a few seats.

Sushi Mania
Via dei Servi 79/r
Tel. 055.211815
11.30am-11pm,
closed Sun

A bright place with a smiling staff, selling sushi boxes prepared by a Japanese restaurant, to take away or eat at the tables in the back. You can also order your own selection. Boxes vary from 6 € to 60 € (party box); Japanese beer 3-3.80 €, cocktails 3.80 €.

Turkuaz
Via dei Servi 65/r
Tel 055.2302373,
noon-2pm/6pm-4.30am

Arab sandwiches and dishes complete with *kebab*, salad, yoghurt and sauces. Avoid the hot sauce unless you have a fire extinguisher on hand. Open until late, so that one can still a sudden pang of hunger at little cost (2 to 5 €).

cious pies and cakes, served throughout the day and late into the night.

Pugi

Viale De Amicis 49/r
Tel 055.669666
Piazza San Marco 10
Tel 055.280981
Via San Gallo 62/r
Tel 055.475975
Closed Sun

Pugi in Viale De Amicis is a historic *focacceria*: youngsters have been gathering here in the afternoon from time immemorial to eat warm focaccia with various fillings, pizza or traditional pastries. Now one can join in this "ritual" also at the other, recently opened shops.

Ice-Cream Parlours

Carabè

Via Ricasoli 60/r, tel 055.289476
In summer open Mon-Sun
9.30am-1am

A friendly place selling own-made Sicilian ice cream (try the pistachio), also delicious *granita*, flavoured with seasonal fruit.

Damiani

Via Burchiello 20/r
Tel 055.2335428
In summer open Mon-Sat
11am-1am, Sun 3pm-1am

An ice-cream parlour off the beaten track, but

beloved by Florentines, who come on hot summer evenings to sit under the white beach parasols, while eating ample portions of delicious ice cream at reasonable prices.

Grom

Via del Campanile 2 (at the corner of Via delle Oche),
tel 055.216158, open until 11pm

In a side-street off Via Calzaiuoli, a Turinese ice-cream parlour basing its success on high-quality ingredients, such as Sicilian pistachios, Piedmotese hazelnuts, seasonal fruit. And for gourmets, cocoa from Gobino, one of Turin's best chocolate makers.

Vivoli

Via Isola delle Stinche 7/r
Tel 055.292334,
closed Mon

Every day dozens of tourists stop at world-famous "Vivoli". Ample choice of traditional and novel flavours.

Confectioners, Bars Chocolate Bars

Dolci e Dolcezze

Piazza Beccaria 8/r
Tel 055.2345458, Tue-Sat
8.30am-8pm, Sun 9am-1pm
(in winter also 4-7.30pm)

Not exactly cheap, but absolutely delicious pas-

tries, cakes and pies. The only drawback: there are no tables where to enjoy these treats at leisure.

I dolci di Patrizio Cosi

Borgo degli Albizi 15/r
Tel 055.2480367, closed Sun

The choice of pastries and sandwiches, freshly made throughout the day, is superb. Small wonder this bar, that has also a few tables, is always crowded.

Donnini

Piazza della Repubblica 15/r
Tel 055.213694, closed Tue

Florentines and tourists flock to this soberly elegant bar to drink an espresso at the counter and eat a little something. But it's difficult to choose among the great variety of pastries and sandwiches.

Gilli

Piazza della Repubblica 36-39/r
Tel 055.213896,
closed Tue

Photographs prove that there was a confectioner by the name of Gilli in this same square as far back as the late 19th century. The present café dates from the 1920s and has perfectly preserved decorations and furnishings, making it the only example of Belle Epoque café still existing in Florence.

Hemingway
Piazza Piattellina 9/r
Tel 055.284781, 4.30pm-1am,
Fri and Sat 4.30pm-2am,
Sun 11.30am-8pm, closed Mon

A café renowned in Florence for its hot cocoa (5-7 €), and its wide selection of coffee (3.50-5 €), teas (5 €), and herbal teas (4 €). Sunday brunch served until 2pm.

La Via del Tè
Piazza Ghiberti 22/r
Tel 055.2344967,
Mon-Sat 9.45am-1.45pm/4-
7.30pm, closed Sun

A tea shop where to taste or just buy teas and herbal teas from all over the world.

Le Giubbe Rosse
Piazza delle Repubblica 13-14/r
Tel 055.212280

Established in 1897, the café owes its name to the red uniforms then worn by the waiters. Its moment of glory was in the first decades of the

20th century, when it became the haunt of avant-garde artists, such as Marinetti, Boccioni, Soffici, Carrà and others. To honour this tradition, literary events and exhibitions are staged to this day.

Mizzica
Via Cavour 93/r
Tel 055.4630868

A confectioner and rotisserie selling all kinds of Sicilian treats: *cassata*, *cannoli* (pastry filled with ricotta and candied fruit), six kinds of *arancini* (savoury rice cakes), marzipan, nougat, and more.

Mr. Jimmy's
Piazza Pitti 6/r
Tel 055.2480999
10am-8pm

Brownies, apple pie, bagels and other typical American bakery products, own-made according to traditional recipes.

Paszkowski
Piazza della Repubblica 6/r
Tel 055.210236, closed Mon

One of the most celebrated cafés in town, declared a National Monument in 1991. Established in 1846, it soon became a renowned *café*

chantant, where literati and artists would gather. Today, one can sit inside or alfresco in the evening and enjoy live music.

Rivoire
Piazza della Signoria 5/r
Tel 055.214412,
closed Mon

Since 1872 Rivoire has been *the* artisan chocolatier in town. Here one can enjoy one of the best cocoas in the world, served in an elegant setting. And from the alfresco tables the view of Palazzo Vecchio is as close as it gets (prices, of course, are in keeping with the ambience!).

Vestri
Borgo degli Albizi 11/r
Tel 055.2340374
closed Sun

This minuscule, friendly chocolatier opened a few years ago and already is – literally – on everybody's lips! Leonardo Vestri sells variously flavoured chocolate ice cream, cocoa, confectionery, nougat: all handmade in their workshop in Arezzo.

Nightlife

Florence has over a hundred venues where to spend a pleasant evening or to party well into the small hours.

Stylish American bars, English (or Irish) pubs, disco bars where one can drink an *aperitivo* and then stay on late into the night, venues with live music, South American rhythms... In summer the nightlife crowd moves to the squares of the town and to other places not usually accessible during colder seasons.

Venues change from year to year, and so, while spending a merry evening with the many Florentines who stand their ground even when the city is sizzling, and obviously with tourists from all over the world, one

also has a chance to discover new corners of the town.

For the latest update on Florentine nightlife one can buy the monthly "Firenze Spettacolo" (text partly in English), that lists all the events of the month.

Info, bookings and tickets for all main events at
Box Office
Via Alamanni 39
(alongside the station)
Tel 055.210804,
fax 055.213112
Tue-Sat 10am-7.30pm,
Mon 3.30-7.30pm,
closed Sun

Birrerias & Pubs

Beloved by Florentines and tourists, they are the ideal places where to drink a beer in good company, in an (almost) typical Irish or English setting.

Cluricane
Piazza dell'Olio 9/r

A tiny, Irish-style pub close to the cathedral. Inside it is rather cramped, but during the warm season they place a few tables outside, in the (car-free) street. Very friendly ambience.

Il Bovaro. Birreria Artigianale
Via Pisana 3/r
(Porta San Frediano)
Tel 055.2207057,
closed Sun

A first-rate microbrewery. The beer, brewed according to traditional methods, comes directly from the great wooden vats proudly displayed in one of the rooms. To go with the excellent beers, traditional dishes from northern Italy. The alfresco tables overlook the majestic Porta San Frediano.

J.J. Cathedral
Piazza San Giovanni 4/r
Tel 055.280260, 10am-3am

A friendly pub extending over two floors. If you are really, really lucky you may find yourself drinking the beer of your life sitting on one of two chairs at a diminutive table on the tiniest of balconies, with the Baptistery seemingly within hand's reach. Cocktails – the most expensive item – are 6 €.

La Rotonda
Via il Prato 10-16
Tel 055.2654644, 7.30pm-1am

Smart English-style pub. Upstairs there is a moderately-priced restaurant and pizzeria. Live music from Wednesday to Sunday.

The Cheers Pub
Via dei Renai 27
Tel 055.245829, from 11am until late into the night

This is the place to come to for an *aperitivo* or later for a beer (the choice is ample), but also for lunch or dinner. Entirely fitted out in wood, alfresco space in the summer, satellite TV for watching sports events.

The Chequers Pub
Via della Scala 7-9/r
Tel 055.287588, 6pm-1.30am, Fri and Sat 6pm-2.30am

Vast English-style pub that serves beer and typical snacks (fish and chips, sandwiches, pastries). Happy hour from 5 to 8pm.

The Fiddler's Elbow
Piazza Santa Maria Novella 7a
Tel 055.215056, Mon-Thu 3pm-1am, Fri 3pm-2am, Sat 2pm-2am, Sun 2pm-1am

Renowned for having been the first "Irish pub" in town, the place is crowded winter and summer with locals, students, and tourists. Four rooms inside and alfresco tables in summer. The walls are covered with bizarre writings and items bought from antiques markets.

The Lions Fountain
Borgo Albizi 34/r
Tel 055.2344412, 6pm-2am

Typical "Irish pub", serving beer and sandwiches, where one can watch all American sports events and, sometimes, Italian football

matches. It attracts great crowds of foreign students and tourists, especially in summer, when one can sit or stand outside in the small, picturesque Piazza San Pier Maggiore.

The Old Stove
Via Pelliceria 2/r
Tel 055.284640, noon-2am

A very friendly pub with a cheerful ambience, in a quiet, car-free street next to Piazza della Repubblica. There is an ample choice of Irish beers and of appropriate dishes, mainly based on fish and potatoes. Traditional furnishings and alfresco tables in summer.

The William Pub
Via Magliabechi 7-9-11/r
Tel 055.2638357, from 6pm until late evening

Vast English-style pub in a quiet street next to Piazza Santa Croce. Ample choice of beers, some of them quite rare.

Cocktail bars & cafés

*N*ot just simple cafés, but places where one can go before dinner for an "aperitivo" (the pre-dinner drink that in its more fashionable version comes with a buffet so rich as to make *dinner redundant) or spend the evening and the best part of the night. In the daytime they often serve breakfast, snacks, some even lunch and dinner.*

Astor

Piazza Duomo 20/r
Tel 055.2399000, 10am-3am,
Sun 5pm-3am

A bar in a superb location, next to the Duomo. Alfresco tables and a huge counter with silvery bar stools. It serves breakfast, lunch and

dinner (including fish dishes) until the late hours, besides the obligatory *aperitivo*-cumbuffet, with finger food and even pasta dishes. Downstairs DJs and live music every night.

Cabiria Café

Piazza Santo Spirito 4/r
Tel 055.215732, 8.30am-2am,
closed Tue

A favourite hangout during the long winter nights and even more so in summer, when the square becomes one of the liveliest in town, attracting crowds of locals and tourists. Open, for breakfast, brunch and after-dinner snacks. Tables outside, with view of the church.

Café Caracol

Via de' Ginori 10/r
Tel 055.211427, from 6pm until late into the night, lunch noon-2.30pm, closed Mon

Caribbean cocktails and Mexican food, such as variously filled *tortillas* and meat *fajitas*. The music matches the ambience, occasionally there is also live music. Very crowded happy hour from 6 to 8pm; dinner served from 7.30pm to midnight.

Caffè La Torre

Lungarno Cellini 65/r
Tel 055.680643,
10.30am-3.30am

Located next to Porta San Niccolò, this place boasts one of the most famous *aperitivo* in town. Securing a seat is no mean feat. There is such an abundance of pasta dishes, sandwiches, and finger food of all kinds, that only the most hardy will dare sit down to dinner afterwards. Live music and DJs, midnight snacks. Scrumptious Sunday brunch (at noon) with live music.

Caffè Pitti

Piazza Pitti 9/r, tel 055.2399863
10am-1am (kitchen open late into the night)

Overlooking Palazzo Pitti, a modish and intimate place where to eat a light

lunch, dinner, or have a drink, perhaps downstairs, where lights are soft and couches velvety. Average price for dinner 30-35 €; set lunch 15 €.

Capocaccia

Lungarno Corsini 12/r
Tel 055.210752, Mon open only for lunch

Smart bistro on the river, patronized by fashionistas. Warm sandwiches and cold plates, delicious desserts. The ideal place for lunch or after dinner.

Cardillac Café

Via degli Alfani 57/r
Tel 055.2343993, 8am-2am,
lunch noon-3.30pm

A bar beloved by students, both local and foreign (the university is just a stone's throw away), because of its cheerful ambience and reasonable prices. Very much crowded at lunchtime (Arab-style sandwiches, focaccia, hamburgers, salads), and for *aperitivo*, thanks also to the happy hour and its innumerable shots.

Dolce Vita

Piazza del Carmine
Tel 055.284595, 5pm-1.30am

"Historic" Florentine nightlife place, established in 1985, patronised

by people from the fashion and arts world. This smart disco bar is the right place for an inspired *aperitivo* (7-9.30pm), a cocktail, a miniconcert. Cheese and salami plates at lunchtime. Parking space in the square.

Eby's Latin Bar
Via dell'Oriolo 5/r
Tel 055.240027, noon-3am

Under the picturesque Arch of San Piero, Eby serves cocktails made from fresh fruit, rum, tequila, fresh fruit juices, to go with sandwiches, salads, and salsa music. Moderate prices and extended happy hour (Mon and Tue all day, Wed, Thu and Fri 6-10pm). A new Eby's has opened recently in Via Palazzuolo 63/r.

Elliot Braun
Via Ponte alle Mosse 117/r
Tel 055.352352
Mon-Fri 10am-4pm, 6pm-2am;
Sat and Sun 6pm-2am

A place that changes as the day progresses: part café, part restaurant, part pub. From 7.30 to 9.30pm "apericena" (an *aperitivo* that amounts to a *cena*, a full dinner), with warm and cold

plates, cocktails 5.00 €. After dinner: parties, music, cabaret, theatre performances.

È una questione di gradi
Via Ponte alle Mosse 35/r
Tel 055.333921, 7pm-midnight,
closed Tue

A tiny place but with a distinctive character. From *aperitivo* time on, genuine foods from Calabria: cheese, salami, vegetables preserved in oil, pastries and liqueurs (all products are also for sale).

Flor
Viale Strozzi 28a/b
(Fortezza da Basso)
Tel 055.475902
7.30am-1am, Sun 6pm-1am

The tiny kitchen continues to provide meals throughout the day: buffet breakfast in the morning; first courses, pizza and salads for lunch and dinner. The wine list has a very fine selection; the *aperitivo* changes constantly and is always very carefully prepared; DJ music, themed nights, and occasional art exhibitions.

Lidò
Lungarno Pecori Giraldi 1
Tel 055.2342726, 12.30pm-2am,
closed Mon

On the banks of the

Arno, a tastefully appointed place: wooden bar counter, minimalist tables and chairs, parquetry floor. They serve *aperitivo* and after-dinner snacks, also lunch and Sunday brunch. In the summer, the garden overlooking the river adds to the charm of the evening.

Moyo
Via dei Benci 23/r
Tel 055.2479738
Open for lunch and after 6pm

Trendy and high-tech (the first *wi fi* place to open in Florence). The softly lighted vast space, full of smart details, fills up for *aperitivo*… and remains crowded for the entire evening!

Negroni Florence Bar
Via de' Renai 17/r
Tel 055.243647, Mon-Sat
8am-2am, Sun 6pm-2am

As a rather dingy bar it figured in a successful

1970s film, "Amici miei". Now refurbished, it serves cocktails and long drinks that one can sip also in the small square close to the Arno. Open throughout the day for breakfast, lunch, *aperitivo*, dinner.

Nova Bar
Via Martelli 14/r

Two bars, pleasant ambience, open for breakfast, lunch, *aperitivo*, dinner, and most importantly, after dinner.

Piccolo Café
Borgo Santa Croce 23/r
Tel 055.2001057, 4pm-2.30am

Small (as the name says) and friendly bar next to Piazza Santa Croce. Frequented mainly, but not exclusively, by gays. In the evening tasty *aperitivo* in a tranquil and relaxed ambience; later on the night livens up, with music and drinks. It also hosts art exhibitions.

Pop Café
Piazza Santo Spirito 18A/r
Tel 055.211201

A small café in Piazza Santo Spirito, very friendly and snug, where one can taste alcoholic and non-alcoholic drinks from organic ingredients, sushi and finger food. Alfresco tables in summer. It also hosts a club promoting the use of alternative vehicles to fight pollution, which every year holds an exhibition to display the latest inventions.

Rex Café
Via Fiesolana 25/r
Tel 055.2480331, 6pm-3am

A lively American bar named after the famed ocean liner Rex, that held the Blue Riband from 1933 to 1935. Start the evening at the circular bar counter for *aperitivo*, with fantastic cocktails (one of the best *mojitos* in town) at very reasonable prices. Stay on for DJ music, hip hop on Thursday, and themed nights every Friday. Also avant-garde art exhibitions.

Slowly
Via Porta Rossa 63/r
Tel 055.2645354
Open for lunch and after 7pm until late into the night (Thu, Fri and Sat dinner 9.30pm-midnight), closed for lunch on Sun

Contemporary design is the trademark of this two-storey place. Long counter at the entrance, and small, coloured couches opposite. The *aperitivo* is delicious (especially on Sunday, when they serve fish), but it's not a bad idea to stay for dinner (Tuscan and multiethnic cuisine), and for the night

(cocktails and music). First courses 7-8 €, specialities 13 €, desserts 3.50 €; buffet lunch 9 €. The works of art are from Ken's Art Gallery in Via Lambertesca.

Tijuana
Via Ghibellina 156-158/r
Tel 055.2341330, 7pm-3am

A restaurant and bar serving aperitifs, cocktails and Mexican dishes. Live music.

Zoe
Via dei Renai 13/r
Tel 055.243111; open from early morning to 1am, Sat until 2am

Trendy, very popular American bar. Crowded particularly at *aperitivo* time (wide choice of cocktails and finger food) and in the before-disco hours, but one can come also for a quick lunch. It opens onto a small square, allowing customers to sip their drink while enjoying some fresh air in summer.

Nightlife

Disco bars

*P*laces that are part restaurant, part bar, part disco... and inevitably crowded!

Maracanà
Via Faenza 4A/r
Tel 055.210298, 8.30pm-4am, closed Mon

A paradise for lovers of South American and especially Brazilian rhythms. The evening starts with a traditional Brazilian dinner, continues with live music, dance or capoeira exhibitions, then with disco into the small hours – and glasses of *caipirinha* and *caipiroska* along the way, of course.

Otel
Via Generale della Chiesa 9
Tel 055.650791,
Thu-Sun 8.30pm-3am

This recently opened place, that calls itself a "ristotheatre", has quickly become one of the most trendy and crowded establishments in town. During dinner there is a show with dancers, magicians, comedians, singers... then live and DJ music late into the night. Large car park.

Salamanca
Via Ghibellina 80/r
Tel 055.2345452
7.30pm-2am

Spanish restaurant and bar, much frequented by foreign students, who tend to linger inside and outside into the small hours. *Tapas* and other typical dishes, to go with wine, beer and *sangría*; *paella* made to order. Evenings with live Latin American music, Spanish dances, or simply karaoke.

Discothèques

Central Park
Via Fosso Macinante 1
(Parco delle Cascine)
Tel 055.353505
closed Mon and Tue

One of the most beloved discos in town. In winter it tends to be somewhat cramped, but in summer one can enjoy the garden and the alfresco dance floor. 70s and 80s, hip hop, and house nights. Saturday and Sunday access is restricted to over 25s.

Jaragua
Via Erta Canina 12/r
Tel 055.2343600

When it opened in 1993, it was the first place in town to be entirely dedicated to Latin music. Salsa and merengue are danced here every evening. There are also dance courses held by professional teachers. And they serve typical Latin American cocktails, of course. A decided plus factor: entrance is free and there is no obligation to order a drink.

Meccanò
Via degli Olmi 1
Tel 055.331371; 11pm-5am, closed Sun and Mon

Located at the entrance to the Cascine, with great windows opening onto the park, this trendy, glamorous place has captured the fancy of Florentine night owls. It boasts a fine bar with a wide selection of drinks, a restaurant, and a discothèque with live music or top-quality Italian DJs. Themed nights Fri and Sat; selection at the door. In summer one can revel outside in the garden.

Tenax
Via Pratese 46, tel 055.632958,
open Fri, Sat and for concerts

One of the most frequented discos in town, boasting top DJs, special

Nightlife

Festival!

This is beyond doubt the main cultural event in Florence. Founded by Italian conductor Vittorio Gui in 1933, the festival quickly reached world fame. Its main focus has always been on rediscovering works and authors from the past, and exploring 20th-century music. It attracts celebrated interpreters, directors and scenographers, and takes place approximately in May-June. Visitors flock to it from all over the world, and it is

Festival dei popoli

Main venue:
Cinema Alfieri Atelie,
Via dell'Ulivo 6
(may change in 2007)
Time: November-December
For over 40 years now, this film festival has been bringing to Florence the best documentary films from all over the world. Every year there is a full week of non-stop afternoon and evening events: crowded film screenings, meetings with authors, debates on the issues raised by the documentaries shown.
Info: Istituto Italiano per il Film di Documentazione Sociale, *Borgo Pinti 82/r*, tel 055.244778, www.festivaldeipopoli.org.

Maggio Musicale

Teatro Comunale
Corso Italia 16
Tel 055.213535
Fax 055.287222

Where to buy tickets:
- Ticket Office: Tue-Fri 10am-4.30pm, Sat 10am-1pm
- Call center tel 199112112, Mon-Fri 8am-8pm, Sat 8am-3pm; tickets sold over the phone will be delivered to the address given (up to 7 days before the performance)
- Tourist Authority offices
- Box Office (see "Tickets")

therefore advisable to book well in advance, especially for premieres.
During the rest of the year, the Teatro Comunale stages opera, ballet and concerts; its summer performances in the superb setting of the Boboli Gardens make for an unforgettable experience.

Musica dei popoli

Auditorium "Flog W Live"
Via Mercati 24
Tel 055.487145; time: October
One of the most important ethnic and folk music festivals to be held in Italy, "Musica dei popoli" has been bringing the musical traditions of the world's peoples to Florence since 1979, attracting artists from every corner of the globe.
Info: Centro FLOG Tradizioni Popolari, *Via Maestri del Lavoro 1 Tel 055.4220300-055.4224276, fax 055.4223241*

guests, a wine bar with sommelier in attendance, and even an art gallery. Throughout the year there are also great concert nights, with renowned Italian and foreign artists.

Yab Yum

Via Sassetti 5/r - Tel 055.215160
(close to Piazza della Repubblica)

This disco, an institution in Florentine nightlife, has kept up to date by changing frequently, with an eye for the newest trends. Its main attractions are the large dance floor, its lighting effects, and the four bars. Themed nights, and DJ music from hip hop, to house, to pop. Tables are around the dance floor, in case one decides to dine before flinging oneself into the dance.

Live music

Auditorium Flog W Live

Via M. Mercati 24
(Poggetto area)
Tel 055.487145

Relaxed, informal ambience, live concerts (rock, reggae, world music), exhibitions of emerging bands, or "alternative" disco nights. Very, very crowded. It is also the venue of the "Musica dei Popoli" festival.

A very special theatre

Teatro del Sale
Via dei Macci 111/r
Tel 055.2001492
9am-3pm/6pm-midnight,
closed Sun and Mon
Booking required

Its creators are Maria Cassi and husband Fabio Picchi (owner of the legendary "Cibreo") and it is a highly imaginative place: part English-style club (with wide armchairs to sink in and newspapers and magazines to leaf through), part restaurant (but at the buffet one has the feeling of being at a party), part theatre (with interesting and novel performances). Entrance is for members only (membership card 10 €, 5 € for young people, pensioners, and temporary visitors) and only after booking. Not more than 99 guests are admitted each night. Breakfast is served from 9 to 11am (5 €), lunch from 12.30 and 2pm (14 €), dinner from 7 to 8.45pm (24 €); the performance begins at 9.30pm.

TEATRO DEL SALE
CIBRÈO CITTÀ APERTA 2002
FIRENZE

CIRCOLO CREATIVO D'INTRATTENIMENTO CULTURALE

Chiodo Fisso

Via Dante Alighieri 16/r
Tel 055.2381290
8pm-2am, closed Sun

Since 1978 a favourite hangout for fans of singer-songwriters and lone performers: solo guitarists, jazz and folk musicians (but Tuesday is hip hop night!). The perfect place for a quiet evening with friends. The membership card is free of charge.

Girasol

Via del Romito 1 G/r
Tel 055.474948,
8pm-3am, closed Mon

A Latin bar with live Caribbean music: rumba, flamenco, also Brazilian and Cuban music, Latin jazz... and with dancing instructors on hand! Cocktails and snacks befitting the place.

Jazz club

Via Nuova de' Caccini 3
(at the corner with Borgo Pinti)
Tel 055.2479700, from 9.30pm
until late into the night, closed
Sun.

A favourite with jazz fans, and not only with them. Sip a beer or a cocktail, to go with finger food and pastries, while listening to live music every night (jazz, world, Brazilian and Cuban). Membership card 6 €.

Porto di mare

Via Pisana 128
Tel 055.715794,
8pm-3am

One can dine pleasantly, with typical Tuscan and Calabrian dishes, or just have a pizza. The place, however, owes its fame to its lively concerts: every night live Italian music, and the stage is always open to artists and bands.

Needless to say, Florence, being one of the main tourist destinations of the world, offers an ample choice of accommodation, ranging from luxury hotel to modest guesthouse. Nevertheless, during the main tourist season (i.e. most of the year), one may encounter problems in finding a room, or at least an accommodation suited to one's wishes. It is therefore advisable to book well in advance.

Consorzio Florence Promhotels
free hotel bookings
freephone 800.866022 (9 am-7 pm, Sat 9 am-1 pm)
www.promhotels.it
e-mail: info@promhotels.it

---

5 stars

Helvetia & Bristol
Via dei Pescioni 2
Tel 055.26651, fax 055.288353
www.hbf.royaldemeure.com

This historic 19th-century hotel, close to Via Tornabuoni, has had many famous personages among its guest, such as D'Annunzio, Pirandello, De Chirico and Stravinskij. Furnished in a very grand style, it has a magnificent winter garden, where the

restaurant and cocktail bar are located. Double room max 750 €.

Regency
Piazza D'Azeglio 3
Tel 055.245247, fax 055.2346735
www.regency-hotel.com

A very tranquil location not far from the centre and close to the ring road (and therefore easy to reach by car). Elegantly furnished, it boasts a fine garden and an excellent restaurant. Single rooms (max 360 €), doubles (max 480 €), and suites (max 840 €).

Villa La Vedetta
Viale Michelangelo 78
Tel 055.681631, fax 055.6582544
www.villalavedettahotel.com

Close to Piazzale Michelangelo, a hotel with only 18 rooms, surrounded by an Italian-style garden and boasting a terrace and an outdoor swimming pool with view of the town.

Doubles (max 980 €) and suites (max 2000 €).

Villa San Michele
Via Doccia 4, Fiesole
Tel 055.5678200, fax 055.5678250
www.villasanmichele.orient-express.com

A 15th century Franciscan monastery on the hill of Fiesole, surrounded by gardens and woods. The façade has been attrib-

early 20th-century building, close to the railway station and to the main tourist attractions. Its 102 rooms (double max 900 €) are tastefully furnished, with selected fabrics. The hotel has a restaurant, an American bar, and a wine bar.

Albergotto
Via Tornabuoni 13
Tel 055.2396464, fax 055.2398108
www.albergotto.com

A historic hotel that has had among its guests many celebrated person-

and used to be a convent. Several rooms have beam ceilings, the breakfast room has pointed arches and Romanesque columns. However, it does not lack modern amenities: bar room, fitness room, internet point. The hotel has an arrangement with a garage across the street. Double max 380 €.

Berchielli
Lungarno Acciaioli 14
Tel 055.264061, fax 055.218636
www.berchielli.it

Ideally located between the Arno and the Medieval "chiassi" (one entrance is from the picturesque Piazzetta del Limbo), it has a fine Art Déco decoration, all the amenities of a luxury hotel and splendid views. Double max 350 €.

uted to Michelangelo. The double rooms (max 1663 €) and suites (max 3000 €) have every kind of amenity, and almost all enjoy a view over Florence. Excellent restaurant and cookery courses.

4 stars

Albani
Via Fiume 12
Tel 055.26030, fax 055.211045
www.albanihotels.com

Located in an imposing

ages, such as Verdi, Donizetti, George Elliot. Recently refurbished, it boasts fine beam ceilings and antique furniture. Double room max 335 €.

Atlantic Palace
Via Nazionale 12
Tel 055.213031, fax 055.268353
www.atlanticpalace.it

One would never guess it from the outside, but the building where this hotel is located dates from the 13th century

Brunelleschi
Piazza S. Elisabetta 3
Tel 055.27370, fax 055.219653
www.hotelbrunelleschi.it

A fairy-tale hotel in a

tiny piazza right in the centre of town, located inside the Byzantine "Torre della Pagliazza" and the church of San Michele in Palchetto, both carefully restored so as to preserve their architectural features. A private museum displays traces of a Roman *calidarium* and Medieval plates. All 96 rooms have a superb view, some overlook the cathedral. Double max 360 €.

Grand Hotel Minerva
Piazza S.M. Novella 16
Tel 055.27230, fax 055.268281
www.grandhotelminerva.com

Located near the railway station, in the centre of town, and overlooking one of its most beautiful squares, the hotel has 103 rooms with all amenities, and view of the church of S. Maria Novella or over a garden. Roof-top swimming pool. Double max 420 €.

Hotel degli Orafi
Lungarno degli Archibusieri 4
Tel 055.26622, fax 055.2662111
www.hoteldegliorafi.it

Halfway between the Uffizi Gallery and Ponte

Vecchio, in an ancient mansion, the hotel has frescoed and coffered ceilings; the ancient Medieval tower, demolished by the Ghibellines, has been partially recovered. The view from the terrace is unique. Double room max 480 €.

Lungarno Hotel
Borgo San Jacopo 14
Tel 055.27261, fax 055.268437
www.lungarnohotels.com

When fashion and hotel industry meet... Ferragamo, a legendary name in Florentine fashion, has recently opened this ultrachic hotel, full of light, art, amenities and elegance. Double max 814 €. **The Gallery Hotel Art** and the **Continentale** also belong to the same "family".

Monna Lisa
Borgo Pinti 27
Tel 055.2479751, fax 055.2479755
www.monnalisa.it.

A charming hotel located in a *palazzo* dating in part from the 14th

century and extensively altered in the 16th, with coffered ceilings, antique furniture and works of art. The palace belonged to the family of St Filippo Neri (who was born here in 1515) and more recently to the family of the neoclassical sculptor Giovanni Dupré (1817-1882), many of whose works can be seen in the hotel. There is also a very fine garden. Doubles max 360 €, suites 720 €. Access to the parking lot is from Vicolo della Pergola, which flanks the theatre by the same name.

Villa Carlotta
Via Michele di Lando 3
Tel 055.2336134, fax 055.2336147
www.hotelvillacarlotta.it

Close to Porta Romana, a friendly, elegant hotel, that also has a restaurant and a bar room. Doubles max 299 €.

3 stars

Annalena
Via Romana 34
Tel 055.222402, fax 055.222403
www.hotelannalena.it

On the piano *nobile*, the principal floor of an ancient *palazzo*, opposite one of the entrance gates to Boboli, and therefore close to Pitti Palace, a quiet hotel overlooking a fine garden. Double max 166 €.

Benivieni
Via delle Oche 5
Tel 055.2382133, fax 055.2398248
www.hotelbenivieni.it

In a picturesque alley behind the cathedral, a small, early 16th-century palace that was used as a synagogue in the first half of the 20th century. Carefully refurbished, it has 15 air-conditioned and soundproofed rooms (but not enough to keep out the pealing of the bells in Giotto's tower), with every amenity. Double max 220 €.

Loggiato dei Serviti
Piazza SS. Annunziata 3
Tel 055.289592, fax 055.289595
www.loggiatodeiservitihotel.it

The building (1517-1527) was commissioned by the Servite Order of nearby SS. Annunziata to Antonio da Sangallo and Baccio d'Agnolo, and was used originally as guest house for church dignitaries visiting Flor-

Residential Hotels

Antica Torre di Tornabuoni Uno
Via Tornabuoni 1
Tel 055.2658161,
fax 055.218841
www.tornabuoni1.com
Twelve rooms furnished with antique furniture on the top floors of a Medieval tower. Some have a balcony, and all enjoy a fine view, which becomes absolutely stunning from the two roof terraces. Italian poets Alessandro Manzoni and Vittorio Alfieri stayed here, also several English noblemen in the late 19th and early 20th centuries. Double max 450 €.

I Colli
Via Michele di Lando 7
Tel 055.229297,
fax 055.223513,
www.icolli.it
A villa dating from 1867, surrounded by a large garden, in an absolutely quiet street a stone's throw from Porta Ro-

mana. There are 14 mini-flats (some inside the villa, some in cottages) with rather basic furnishings, to very moderate prices (two people 79-110 €).

Palazzo Magnani Feroni
Borgo San Frediano 5
Tel 055.2399544,
fax 055.2608908
www.florencepalace.it
Luxury residential hotel in a 16th-century aristocratic palace, with 12 suites, salon, bar, billiard room, gym and a large terrace overlooking the town. Double max 900 € (breakfast included).

Palazzo Niccolini al Duomo
Via dei Servi 2, tel 055.282412
fax 055.290979
www.niccolinidomepalace.com
The hotel, practically adjoining the Duomo, and entirely renovated, maintains the feel of an aristocratic mansion, thanks also to the opulent furnishings and the painted ceilings. Double 215-600 €, suite 500 € (breakfast included).

This recently refurbished hotel is close to the railway station and to the main monuments and museums. All rooms have en-suite bathrooms, air conditioning and a safe. There are also a bar room, a reading room, a large breakfast room, and an internet point. Guests can use one of several garages that have an arrangement with the hotel. Double 65-150 € (breakfast included).

ence. In the late 19th century it was sold to private buyers, who used it as an inn. Extensive restoration work carried out in the 1980s brought back to light the original structure. The antique furniture (including four-poster beds) and the view from the windows add to the charm of this very fine hotel. Double max 220 €.

Villa Fiesole
Via Beato Angelico 35
Tel 055.597252, fax 055.599133
www.villafiesole.it

Quiet, elegant hotel in a 19th-century villa, surrounded by typical Tuscan vegetation. The pleasant rooms (max 220 €) overlook Florence. The view from the terrace is superb, and there is also a swimming pool.

2 stars

Accademia
Via Faenza 7
Tel 055.293451, fax 055.219771
www.accademiahotel.net
www.hotelaccademiafirenze.com

Azzi
Via Faenza 56
Tel 055.213806,
fax 055.2398322
www.hotelazzi.com

A pleasant inn in an ancient palace. The rooms have antique or retro furniture, and each one is different from the others. The living room boasts a fireplace, a small library, and board games. Double 70-110 €, a light break-

fast included. On the third floor are some shared rooms (bed per night 20-27 €, buffet breakfast included).

Casci
Via Cavour 13
Tel 055.211686,
fax 055.2396461
www.hotelcasci.com

A small, family-run hotel in a 15th-century palace where Gioacchino Rossini lived for some time. The rooms are well equipped, and in the hotel's bar room there is a free internet point for guests. Buffet breakfast is served in a room decorated with frescoes. Double 90-150 € (breakfast included).

Centro
Via Ginori 17
Tel 055.2302901, fax 055.212706
www.hotelcentro.net

The hotel was entirely refurbished in 1996 and is located in a Renaissance palace where no less a person than Raphael lived at some time. Rooms are decorated in Florentine style,

Accommodation

HOTEL
CENTRO
★★

with original paintings, and have telephone, TV and a safe. Cars can be parked in nearby garages by arrangement with the hotel. Double 95-140 € (breakfast included).

Decò
Via Panzani 7
Tel 055.284469,
fax 055.2302847
www.hoteldeco.it

This centrally located hotel has bright rooms with en-suite bathroom, air conditioning, TV and telephone. The bar room is open 24 hours a day; laundry service is available on request. Double with bathroom max 150 € (lavish buffet breakfast included).

La Scaletta
Via Guicciardini 13
Tel 055.283028,
fax 055.289562
www.lascaletta.com
www.hotellascaletta.it

A small, family-run hotel on the top floor of a 15th-century palace, with two terraces affording a fine view. Double with bathroom 85-150 € (breakfast included).

Villani
Via delle Oche 11
Tel 055.2396451,
fax 055.215348
www.hotelvillani.it

On the 4th floor of a building in an alley right behind the cathe-

VILLANI
★★

dral, a rather basic hotel, but with absolutely breathtaking panoramas from nearly most of its windows. Double max. 120 €, quadruple max. 200 €.

1 star

Il Perseo
Via Cerretani 1
Tel 055.212504,
fax 055.288377
www.hotelperseo.it

A guesthouse close to the Duomo, with spacious, bright rooms, fine view, and also a breakfast room and a bar. A nearby garage can be used by agreement. Double without bath 60-73 €, with bath 95 €; breakfast included.

Regina
Borgo la Noce 8
Tel 055.292346,
fax 055.291035
www.hotelreginafirenze.it

A small hotel in the centre of town: 8 double rooms, with or without en-suite bathroom. Bar room and reception open 24 hours a day. The reception will also book tickets to the main museums for guests. Double with bath 90 €, without bath 70 €; breakfast included.

Camp sites

Camping with a view
Viale Michelangelo 80
Tel 055.6811977,
fax 055.689348
www.ecvacanze.it
If you camp, do it here: close to the town centre, with a superb view and within walking distance of the town (public transport available). The bar has a terrace overlooking the town, there are a supermarket and all the usual facilities. Open throughout the year.